"*Mosaic* is beautiful, absolutely beautiful! Oh, how could anything be more poignant than trying to reach our children? They are there waiting to emerge like butterflies from their cocoons. I have been on the edge of the precipice with my own child and I know. The poem *Ordinary Divinity* reminds me so much of Ann Morrow Lindberg's retreat to the sand and sea to replenish herself so she could go on with life. Moms need to be inspired when we feel that we just don't have the strength to go on."

—**Elaine Gottschall**, B.A., M.Sc., Author, *Breaking the Vicious Cycle*, and mother of a daughter healed of ulcerative colitis by the *Specific Carbohydrate Diet*

"A beautiful aspect of this book is that it will let other parents know that they are not alone with their challenges or in their fears and worries. And, ultimately, it offers them a path so that they too can build a world around their child that is wonderful and magical."

—**William Hogan**, Executive Director of Programs, *Autism Treatment Center of America,* and father of a daughter diagnosed with autism now functioning typically

"I feel enlightened, empowered, and emotionally renewed after such meaningful words. Reading *Mosaic* is like watching the movie of a soul play before me. These stories capture the raw emotion behind working with autistic children. They have me thinking more about every little thing—in and out of the therapy room. I can't wait to give this book to everyone I know!"

—**Julie Gayler**, Behavioral Therapist, teacher, and mother of a typically developing son

"I read the book cover to cover with a box of tissues by my side. What Elizabeth has done is so important. It is a gift to all of us who have taken a similar journey. It gives poetic voice to the struggles, the triumphs, and the things we dare not say. It gives voice to the loneliness, the fear, the isolation, and, ultimately, to the revelation that we are the blessed ones. It is a masterpiece."

—**Linda Mullen**, J.D., Attorney and mother, whose legal skills enabled her to win ABA therapy funding for her son diagnosed with a non-verbal learning disorder now functioning well in mainstream schooling

"When I read the poem *Black Water,* I was nearly floored by it! The images in roots and water and being drunk with

her babies. Oh, how indescribably power

—**Lisa Murphy**, Writer and mother of typica

"Elizabeth is truly gifted to capture the emotions of parenting an ASD child so well. Her poems brought tears not just to my eyes, but to my heart. It is so comforting to know that others are going through the same horrible, wonderful journey."
—**Sue Swanson**, Mother of a son diagnosed with autism

"*Mosaic* has touched the deepest part of my soul. So many times I experienced the same fears, joys, sorrows, anger, and confusion. And I too can't believe we have our son when many times I thought all was lost."
—**Jenifer Westphal**, Founder, *Kyle's Treehouse*, an autism support site, and mother of a son diagnosed with autism now functioning typically

"I can only imagine the release and moments of epiphany when others read this and think, "YES! This is what I'm feeling!" and then shed some tears of familiarity that have been anxious to roll. This work is important for parents and children with typical struggles—not only for those who have extra-ordinary challenges. Who among us has not felt the uncertainty of our parenting and our choices? Who has not wondered if we are reaching our children? Who among us has not wished to revert to our childhood for a rescue from our parents? These are universal themes which reinforce the concept that we are more alike than we are different."
—**Shawna Butler**, Mother of typically developing children

"Wow! Elizabeth's words are put together so powerfully and efficiently. I haven't cried so deeply in a while. I am truly touched. Being a mother of a child who is not typical makes you so emotionally vulnerable and Elizabeth expressed that in a way few others could."
—**Ronna Davis**, Mother of a son diagnosed with autism

"Elizabeth dares to speak the truth. It is terribly difficult to convey the conflicting feelings involved in raising a special needs child. *Mosaic* delivers this with grace, passion, and brutal honesty."
—**Dara Fairgrieves**, Mother of a daughter diagnosed with a developmental coordination disorder

"Elizabeth has found a way to put something I thought was indescribable into words. Thank you for giving voice to the feelings of heartbreak, confusion, fear, and even triumph that I too have experienced over the past seven years."
—**Carmen Simons**, Mother of a son diagnosed with autism

A Long Way from Shattered Glass to

Mosaic

Living with Autism Spectrum Disorder

A Journaling Memoir

Elizabeth Newman

Published by
Living Mosaic Publishing
2451 Cumberland Parkway, Suite 3312
Atlanta, Georgia 30339-6157

www.livingthemosaic.com

First Paperback Edition
2008

Ten-digit ISBN: 0-9816533-0-8
Thirteen-digit ISBN: 978-0-9816533-0-3

Library of Congress Control Number: 2008925797

Cover and interior layout designed by Elizabeth Newman, Jody Daniel Newman, Julie Gayler, Carmen Simons, and Dara Fairgrieves with art work by Julie Kessler, cover graphics support by Kip Williams, and interior formatting provided by the endlessly patient Kimberly Martin.

"Beloved"

Cover art taken from this original mosaic by Julie Kessler

Julie discovered her love for creating art 13 years ago when she left her medical career to become a stay-at-home mom for her daughter, Audra Lee, who has autism and cerebral palsy. Like many families with an autism diagnosis, heart break, lost dreams, and a terrifying future are just the beginning of autism's storm. Julie's art helped her make it through many truly tough times. Her studio has become her therapy room, allowing her a place and time to heal. Here she creates mosaics of the unexpected treasures Audra has brought to her life.

Julie has developed and taught mosaic classes for mothers of special needs children and dreams of having an art center and gallery where families with disabilities can have an opportunity to express themselves.

www.BlueTangoArtFactory.com
or email Julie at
juliekesslerart@cfl.rr.com

"By His mighty power at work within us,
He is able to accomplish infinitely more
that we would ever dare to ask or hope."

Ephesians 3:20

This collection of stories
is dedicated
to my daughters.

Kate
Sophie
Gabrielle
Mia

They are my constant inspiration
and unwitting teachers.

To each I owe so much,
for they have enlarged my life
in ways
I never dreamt possible.

Acknowledgements

Mia is one child we have needed many hands to raise. We have had much help from above and from so many earthly angels. For all these caring hearts, I send my humble thanks.

To my husband, Jody Daniel Newman, his steady love, integrity, humor, intellect, and dedication hold up our family and our home. He makes the difficult bearable, the mundane comical, and the triumphant blissful. It is, without question, only through his enthusiastic support that this publication came together.

To my beautiful daughters, Kate, Sophie, and Gabrielle, their determined spirits, love for Mia, and lively involvement in her therapy program are such blessings. And to Mia, for she continues to teach me more than I ever imagined there was to learn.

To my parents, Dr. James and Greta Kelso, for, well, just about everything. Their tenacious wills, enduring faith, and gracious forbearance have been lifelong inspirations to me. Even I do not fully comprehend the great debt I owe them.

To my very dear mother-in-law, Patricia Newman, she has made so much room for us in her life and has greatly enriched each of ours. And to my father-in-law, Ken Newman, for the time he spends "Mia-whispering."

To my sisters, Leslie Teeling, Karen Monette, Marianne Kelso, Suzanne Schulte, and to my brothers, David Kelso and James Kelso, for being a special part of the grand, disastrous, and sometimes misguided segments of my journey. As every year marches on, I increasingly appreciate each of them.

To Jill Kelso, Madeline Monette, Jeff and Debbie Newman, Jason and Jeanne Newman, Jenine Newman, Paul Schulte, Joe Teeling, and to each amazing person in my large and wonderful family of in-laws, nieces, nephews, aunts, uncles, cousins, and grandparents for prayers, hugs, laughs, and welcoming Mia as a wacky and cherished part of our tribe.

To Jeff and Traci Abel, when I would leave Mia at the hospital with Jody, late in the evening, to spend a few hours at home, I would hear stories about this wonderful couple who lovingly played, shared meals, and read with my girls.

To Dara Fairgrieves and Roya Memar, whose enthusiasm for this project and support in surviving the emotional and practical realities of mothering our uniquely challenged children is priceless.

To Thomas and Kerri Kosse, they raised the possibility of hope long before I had seen it myself. They've traveled a path similar to ours and continue to encourage us.

To Linda Mullen, she ventured before me down the road of autism and graciously handed me her guidance. Her brilliance, determination, and delicious wit gave me the courage to move each inch forward as she cheered me every step of the way.

To Lisa Murphy, her soulful camaraderie as a writer and confidant helped guide my thoughts and pen. She is my fountain of honest intellectual and emotional assessment, literary critique, and heartfelt commiseration.

To Lisa and Billy Schlosser, so many of their words were just what I needed as we laughed, cried, mourned, and celebrated together. They also gave freely of their musical inspiration and participation in recording "Hey, Little One."

To Carmen Simons, whose friendship, faith, insight, and humor, as we mother our very unusual children, are invaluable, and whose initiative and propensity for conceptual brilliance put the final and magical touches on this book. With her input, this work found its place.

To Jen Westphal, her gentle sharing of the journey with her autistic son set me on a new path with my own daughter. She is unstoppable in her mission to create awareness and give hope to all whose lives are touched by autism. Our stories are shared.

To the Cahill, Gaskin, Guarisco, Jones, Mendoza, Rowe, Ramaswamy, Sharfstein, Spellissy, Suzuki, Wagner, and Vinings Estates Swim Team families, as well as to Graham Fowler and each member of my *Peachtree Yoga Teacher Training* class, all these people and many more friends and acquaintances have kept us in their thoughts, rendered us kindnesses both tangible and healing, and provided a refuge of comforting words.

To Dr. Ivar Lovaas, who defined the *Applied Behavioral Analysis* techniques. And to Dr. Stanley Greenspan for his *Floor-time Approach.* Their programs were our first lines of hope.

To the wonderful Elaine Gottschall for her work with the *Specific Carbohydrate Diet* and the profound benefits she found it could provide for children with autism and epilepsy.

To all the brilliant, loving, creative, and dedicated people of the *Autism Treatment Center of America's Son Rise Program* for showing us how to reach Mia. The work they do is such a gift to every family they enfold.

To Judith Bluestone, who created the *HANDLE Institute* to teach *Gentle Enhancement* therapy. Judith was the first to truly understand Mia's sensory and neurological needs. She also generously agreed to write the perfect foreword for this book.

To the founders and staff of *Kyle's Treehouse*, *Autism Speaks*, *Autism Society of America, Believe In Me, Jacob's Ladder, Summit Learning Center*, and *Myles-A-Part* for working to increase autism awareness, resources, and support.

To Dr. Jeffrey Abrams, Dr. Jacqueline Hrivnak, and Dr. John Hicks, they took the time to understand our concerns, read our research, and work with us toward healing our daughter.

To Drs. Fernhoff, Saripkin, Pilzer, Meyers, Poulin, Janus,

George-Bussey, Garbacz, Aaron, and all the doctors who worked with Mia, especially to the gifted Dr. John Freeman for his insightful handbook written for parents of children with epilepsy.

To Carole Huotari of La Leche League, Father Caffrey of St. Thomas Church, Lisa Mellgren and Shannon Ujvagi of Scottish Rite, and the many wonderful clergy, technicians, therapists, and nurses who supported us during Mia's hospitalizations.

To Mia's angels—they each made a profound mark on the heart of every member of our family. I send my deep thanks to Stella Monko, who has been in this with us since the very beginning, Julie Gayler, who was simply brilliant in her work with Mia and in this book project , LaTisha Styles, Meena Khowaja, Tamara Ringgard, Jaclyn Mori, and Matt Gayler, who stay so vividly a part of our lives, as well as Jess, Alison, Gail, Marianna, Anderson, Adrianna, Melissa, Katy, Vera, Angela, Jessica, Tom, Kristi, Megan, William, Aaron, Chuck, Maretta, Lynette, Teresa, Shuki, Traci, Anna, Kelly, Margo, Tangelia, Jennifer, Tiffany, Mackenzie, Tammy, Connie, Erica, Jennifer, Jessica, Christina, Constance, Jeff, Andrea, Katherine, Kimberly, Tamika, Maliha, Brandi, Kimberly, Meghan, Paula, John, Anna, Ali, and Durgah.

And special thanks to Mia's littlest angels, Cydney and Jordan Abel, Chloe and Emily Cahill, Tias Kosse, Sammi and Mia Mendoza, and Patrick Spellissy for being pivotal role models in Mia's social development. This has not always been an easy task, and I marvel at their compassion.

To Beverly Parks and her staff at Nickajack Elementary, especially Debra Bianchi, Amanda Newman, and Alicia Butler, as well as Kenyatta, Veena, Lillie, Teresa, Shannon, Stephanie, Jennifer, Michele, Jaime, Eric, Catie, Nicole, and Mia's Mighty Multiage classmates for working diligently to develop, participate in, and enhance a successful inclusion program for Mia.

And to all the courageous and determined families of the autism community for sharing their stories.

Foreword

In recent years, with the sudden and daunting upsurge in diagnosed cases of autism, I am frequently asked, "Why do you think there is so much autism today?" I know the person asking this question wants me to tell them "The Cause" of this epidemic, and then, of course, they want me to tell them what "Therapy" will most help achieve "The Cure." As *Mosaic* so powerfully describes, however, the factors that bring on autistic behaviors are many and varied and the cure is elusive. Yet, I welcome the opportunities to answer this question because I see this rise in autism as a call to recognize what truly is most important in this life: human connection.

Consider for a moment that perhaps the failure of any single theory to prove uniquely correct in understanding autism, and the inability of any therapeutic approach to have universally positive effects on every autistic individual, are messages meant to bring us a more sustainable awareness of our own humanity. For it has been a profoundly staggering discovery, bringing many to their knees in disbelief, to uncover that a person thought mentally impaired due to odd behaviors and lack of speech has the mental acuity to write poetry or type out her deepest desires. It causes us to consider those with autism in a new light, realizing these individuals have their own ways of taking in and relating to their world that may, in fact, have something very useful indeed to teach us about how we look at our own lives.

Without such a perspective of possibility, our shortsightedness and adherence to definitions of "typical" behaviors cause some, who have taken up the challenge of diagnosing autism, to unintentionally leave families defeated and hopeless in the pronouncement of a diagnosis. It is crucial for professionals who have studied basic neurodevelopment in their training to explain its basic principle to families. That concept, called neuroplasticity, provides so much needed hope—not false hope in any sense for sixty years of recorded evidence has shown to the neuroscientific community that the brain and our nervous systems are in a constant state of change, adapting to our environments internally (nutrition, digestion, and respiration, as well as our very private aspirations and inspirations) and externally (toxins, music, sounds, lighting, fabrics, social structure, electromagnetic fields, and more).

Neuroplasticity includes an acceptance of synaptogenesis—the creation of new neural connections as our experiences pulse through our bodies and our brains begging us to hold onto useful connections and build ever stronger pathways. Knowledge of this also leads to dismissal of the thought that there are critical stages in development and replaces that concept with the idea of optimal stages of development. Yes, it would be easier for most of us if everyone learned to talk by the age of two or three, but just because someone hasn't begun to speak or converse by the age of seven or ten does not mean that she may not begin to speak at the age of nineteen or even forty-two.

The current and welcomed push toward research in understanding causes and interventions is certainly needed, but what the autism explosion most demands from us is hopeful acceptance. Not the sort of acceptance associated with disinterested tolerance, but true nonjudgmental and appreciative acceptance of autism's behavioral quirks. It is only with this type of acceptance that one can recognize the gifts to be found in that quirky behavior—real individual gifts.

The key to developing this kind of acceptance is the understanding that autistic behaviors *are* communication. If in our discomfort in observing certain behaviors we try to control them arbitrarily with medication or behavioral therapies before we have understood what the behaviors are communicating, we are performing a disservice both to those of us with autism and to those who will then be deprived of sharing the beauty and the fears of an autistic life experience.

As a youngster, I demonstrated almost every autistic behavior recorded: self-stimming by jumping, climbing, moving my hands in front of my eyes in strange patterns, self-injurious behavior, echolalia, obsessive-compulsive rituals, spinning objects incessantly, tapping, chewing my clothes, avoiding eye-contact, flipping through pages in books, avoiding most social interactions, exhibiting strange reactions to certain foods and smells, as well as reacting seriously to the first rendition of the vaccinations for measles, to name a few. But in the 1940s and 50s there was no diagnosis for people like me. So while I was allowed to be part of society, I was, at the same time, judged as weird, stubborn, and immature despite my inherent intellectual gifts.

With only the best of intentions, out of both duty and love, my mother sought out every test and treatment for my unusual behaviors and seizure disorders. She diligently administered medications, nursed my many illnesses and injuries, and acquired speech and psychological consultations for me. Her hope was that I would become "normal!" Out of obligation, she read my poetry in which I poured out my soul—my darkest thoughts and my giddy retreats, and she said, "That's nice," insensitive to the depth of emotion I could share in writing but not voice. She wanted me to relate to her and others as my older sister had, with social grace. She wanted me to have friends and not seclude myself in my own private world of poetry, puzzles, and pogo sticks. To her dying day, my mother never really saw me. She admired some of my accomplishments and certainly recognized my quirks, but could not "know" me.

If I had been born sixty years later, my behaviors would have been recognized and diagnosed as symptoms of autism. And with the recent realization that there is not one isolated reason for someone to have an autistic life experience, as well as all the therapies and holistic perspectives on learning and healing, the availability of networks of other mothers facing the same issues with their children, and a book such as *Mosaic*, my mother could have seen me. And if she had truly seen me, we both could have grown in that process, grown together and grown in our own individual capabilities to accept others with all of their differences and to love each other despite, or even because of, those differences.

This is why I am delighted for those families now in the throes of understanding how to deal with an autistic child or adult that, in *Mosaic*, Elizabeth has bravely exposed herself and her family in all of their frailties and in doing so has shown us their tremendous strength. Their strength came from a desire to view Mia as a wholly able person and to find the beauty in her very unusual approach to life. This is strength we can all appreciate, the strength to be humble, to accept what we cannot understand, to know it is part of the grand design, and more importantly to deeply know that it truly is alright.

Judith Bluestone
Neurodevelopmental/Educational Therapist
Developer of the HANDLE® approach
The HANDLE Institute International, LLC
Author, *The Fabric of Autism: Weaving the Threads into a Cogent Theory*
Winner of the 2004 Jacqueline Kennedy Onassis Award

Preface

Our youngest daughter, Mia, developed epilepsy and autism in the spring of 2001. She did not learn to walk until nearly age two and only began speaking near age four. Today at eight, she has neurological, fine motor, sensory, speech, social, and academic challenges. It has been a torturous, comical, and surprisingly rewarding journey. But we still have so far to go and there are many families who have even longer roads ahead.

Autism is a complex neuro-gastro disorder that inhibits a child's ability to communicate, respond to surroundings, form relationships, handle sensory input, and process food or medicine. In addition, autism can be accompanied by other issues such as cerebral palsy and epilepsy.

The struggles felt by families of autistic children are very real. These children generally do not look different in any physical way but their behaviors can appear manic and bizarre. They typically have no concrete understanding of social dynamics or customs. They often can not speak well, if at all, or express appropriate emotions. They are typically behind in most major developmental milestones. Dealing with a child whose needs are so difficult to decipher, whose behaviors are so difficult to predict, puts a strain on the entire family, often making family outings an impossibility. The even bigger challenge is finding the right people to work with our children in an effective and caring manner.

Until recently, there were few medical or educational professionals to support families as they searched for treatments. Thanks to growing awareness this is beginning to change and medical professionals are arming themselves with a list of treatment options to offer parents. But for the most part the ball remains squarely in the parents' court as we wade through the confusing and costly cornucopia of therapeutic approaches.

As the parent of a child with autism, I remember well my

frantic search for the stories of others traveling this path. And there are countless others walking in my shoes, for worldwide there are an increasingly alarming number of children diagnosed with autism spectrum disorders. In the United States alone, there are more than 1.77 million recorded cases of autism, with a new case being diagnosed every 20 minutes. Estimates are that 1 in every 150 children will be on the spectrum. Autism is the fastest growing childhood epidemic, more prevalent than childhood diabetes, cancer, and AIDS combined. Consequently, in addition to therapeutic advancements, there is a great need to understand the impact such a diagnosis has on families and to create meaningful ways to support them. One of the surest ways to do this is to share our stories.

If you are the parent of a child with autism, I hope, in reading this journaling memoir, you will find the release these words have given me. And where you keenly feel the truth of a sentiment, perhaps you will feel moved to pour out your own heart in the margins, on the journaling pages, or to the heavens. If you are a friend or support person of a family facing autism, I hope reading these stories will help you gain a deeper compassion for the daily issues facing so many of us.

Life challenges us all, and when we find ourselves surrounded by the fragments trauma creates of our once whole lives, it truly is a long way from shattered glass to mosaic. In our own time, we must pick up and place each pain-filled piece purposefully, with an appreciation for the irregularities, which so greatly enhance the masterpiece. In laying out your own life's design, I wish you each nimble hands and artful eyes.

Elizabeth

TABLE OF CONTENTS

Part One: To Just Be Home ______________ *1*

Ferocious Diagnosis ______________ **2**

Black Water ______________ **5**

Stay ______________ **8**

Lowered Spectacles ______________ **14**

Mamamia ______________ **17**

Ordinary Divinity ______________ **22**

Kisses and Band-aids ______________ **25**

Home ______________ **32**

The Not Knowing ______________ **36**

On The Spectrum of Disorder ______________ **39**

Categorical Panoply ______________ **44**

The Merry Band ______________ **48**

How Do I ______________ **52**

Enough ______________ **55**

Covering The Bases ______________ **57**

Hey, Little One ______________ **59**

Denial ______________ **63**

Paths ______________ **67**

Part Two: Spoonfuls of Possibility ________ *69*

You ________ 70
Interruption ________ 73
Choose Again ________ 78
Possibility ________ 81
Lessons ________ 84
The Cloak You Wear ________ 87
Modifications ________ 91
Swat ________ 95
Retreat ________ 98
Perceptions ________ 100
Weary Feet ________ 103
Worry-Free Child ________ 107
Octopus Mom ________ 111
WHACK ________ 114
Your Cell ________ 118
Where Do They Go ________ 122
Smooth and Jagged Treasure ________ 125
Those Who Went Before Me ________ 129

Part Three: Breathing Deep ___________ *131*

The Bridge ___ **132**
Little Muse ___ **135**
On The Mountain ___ **139**
Just Say Yes ___ **142**
Wise Women ___ **147**
Crazy ___ **151**
The Sensation of Things ___ **154**
Wild Thing ___ **158**
Compassion ___ **162**
Stepping Into Your World ___ **164**
Simple Joys ___ **170**
Just Keep Seeking ___ **173**
Even Now ___ **177**
Something More than Happiness ___ **180**
Can This Be True? ___ **185**
Silk and Thorns ___ **189**
Hush ___ **193**

Part One: To Just Be Home

"How long must I wrestle with my thoughts and have sorrow in my heart?"

Psalm 13:2

Ferocious Diagnosis

Macrocytic Anemia
Fifteen months old
B12 Depletion
Halted growth
"Deficient diet,"
We're told

Cobalamin injections
Hydroxo prescribed
Myoclonic Tremors
Writhing movements
Reactions
Well disguised

Side effects
Overdosed
"Could be Cystic Fibrosis."
Spinal Tap
Antibiotics
Septic Leukocystosis

NG Tubes
Losing weight
Stumping every physician
Reactive Airway Disease
Pre-asthmatic Condition

CAT Scan
MRI
Video EEG
Microcephalic
Reduced White Matter
Cerebral Atrophy

Epilepsy
Complex Partials

"Treat with Ativan NOW."
Catatonic
Teeth grinding
Worsened somehow

Genetic testing
IV drips
Low Muscle Tone
Spiking fevers
Partial Deafness
"She'd be best off at home."

Motor skills
Fine and gross
Severely behind
Lack of speech
Retardation
"What more can they find?"

Rigid habits
Flat affection
Gastro Dysfunction
Fleeting eyes
Banging head
Reaching a junction

Hands on ears
Screaming voice
Throwing the puzzle
Sensory fear
Violent slaps
"Just a few of her troubles."

One last label
For the list
On that memorable day
ASD tendencies
And Pervasive Delay

Black Water

"It is nothing you have done."

The very words
summon tears
welling up
from the deep pool
of my uncertainty

What is this spring
feeding icy black water
to my soul

Is it the rain of motherhood
falling almost unnoticed
on the mountain of my worries
trickling down
over years of worn and caring paths
gathering
in the thirsty reservoir of my strength
that I will never run dry
of ways to nurture my seedlings

Such sentient saplings
sprung up
from my soil
how the roots of this love
grow deep in my heart

I long to beat down
like a hot sun
draining the pond of my doubts
licking up the accusing liquid
drop
by drop
yet these same waters
quench a greedy thirst

as I drink up the miracle
of my blossoming babes

With my arms wrapped tight
around small bodies
I inhale their intoxicating scent
and am drunk
flooded
with a fierce instinct
to protect

It is the mortar of my sanity
to know for my dear ones
I have chosen well

So I listen to this echo
tunneling through my veins
I tuck its tone in every crack
to keep my bricks
from crumbling

I seal in its affirmation
and bathe my wounds
in its music

I cling to
and reject it
for of course
I would never
cause my darlings harm

And yet
I need these words

"It is nothing you have done."

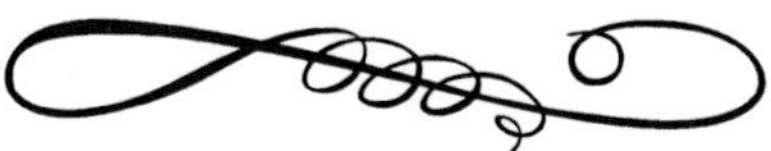

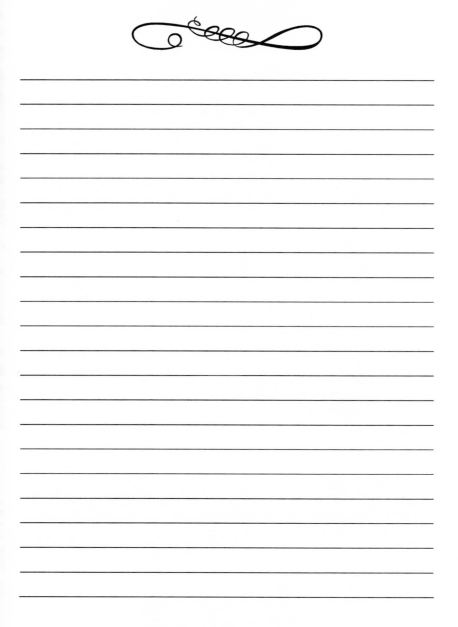

Stay

You were unexpected.

Content at 40
with three girls grown from babyhood
to increasing independence,
I had threaded time
for different journeys.

But you
had other plans for me,
swelling in my belly
as I pitched to and fro
riding waves of escalating nausea,
steadied only by visions of a dark haired babe
whispering her name.

Weeks past due,
content in your amniotic sea,
as if in the last minutes
you second guessed your entrance.
I summoned courage for both of us,
laboring two days,
coaxing,
pleading
for you to choose
"come."

Catching you up against my breast,
I wept tears of joy,
relief.
At last,
my prophetic daughter
so daintily crowned in black.
And with your name
all sweetness on my tongue,
my heart claimed you as its own.

You delighted us all
with the delicate smallness of your features,
but over time something odd
encircled you.
Visible one moment,
fleeting the next,
so that I never quite
found the words for it.

Small things began to concern me,
reflux,
disinterest in food,
popping joints,
slackening muscle tone.
And then just past your first birthday
you slowed noticeably,
ceasing to gain weight,
losing words,
staring off for hours
into vacant space.

We were advised you were a bit anemic
and tried cajoling you,
in vain,
to swallow the iron drops.
Finally,
it was your insipid demeanor
and the complete disappearance of your smile
that sent us scurrying
to the emergency room
in calamitous distress.

Even there
the attending physician speculated
you just needed more iron
as you roused yourself,
grabbing at his stethoscope,
appearing once again

to be a perfectly normal,
though tiny,
one year old.

We were all shocked
when the doctor flew into the room
announcing lab results
showing you to be dangerously depleted
in B12.

It was recommended
that we start a protocol schedule
of several supplemental shots.
We were assured
there were no side affects
and you received your first needle
that very day.
I too asked for an injection
to strengthen my milk,
the only nourishment
you would consume.

The liquid cure took effect quickly.
By evening
we were both cruising along
on a hospital high.
I was sleepless and agitated.
You were transformed
into a babbling bundle of movement,
crawling back and forth
over my wakeful body.

By morning
you appeared so energetic
that we were released
with counsel
to continue the treatments
at home.

But three hours later,
with the entire family
piled on our king size bed
to marvel at your recovery,
your right hand began to shake violently.
The tremor
worked up your arm with frightening speed
and we rushed you back
to the specialists.

Seizure,
a dark and foreign word,
was thrown at us with frantic alarm.
Again we were advised
to puncture your small form
with another
hypodermic medication.

I was hesitant
reasoning that the initial shots
had taken you from stillness
to chaos
and concerned about the effect
yet another medicinal course
might induce.
I climbed into your metal-railed bed
speaking softly to you,
quieting your quake,
wrapping myself around you
like a fortress
holding off a new assault.

Dawn ushered in an outraged,
though compassionate,
neurologist.
She insisted
on immediate treatment.
Her manner

won your father
and he urged me
to leave the floor
so anti-seizure medication
and brain activity monitoring
could be administered.

On my return
you had become mush,
more lethargic and feeble
than at the start of this ordeal.
Looking at you
so swallowed up in tubes and tape,
I began to weep silently,
every tear a plea
addressed to your comatose form.

For though you entered my womb
unanticipated,
I welcomed you.
And when you resisted
leaving that safe place,
I called you forth
in happy expectation.

You hover now between absence
and living fully here,
but do not be afraid.
There is a place for you,
a life of possibilities.
I will make room for you
despite my fears.
You have only to release yours
and know I will be here
standing near,
waiting
for you to choose
"stay."

Lowered Spectacles

You tried to convince me
I was a foolish mother,
harming my child
through stupidity
or neglect.

I tried to convince myself
I was a good mother,
who could learn
from my mistakes,
and I asked
for proof
of your theory.

You lowered your spectacles
and glared at me
like I was a thorn
poised to punch a hole
in your tidy diagnosis.

I stood resolute,
patient but firm,
while you ordered the test
I had requested.

You went home
and closed your eyes,
certain of the outcome,
prepared for another
"I told you so" lecture
to a dimwitted parent.

I stayed,
swallowed
under the hospital sky,
torn,

wanting you
to be right
for frightening possibilities
lurked in the shadow
of your error.

You arrived in the morning
with test results and apologies,
erroneously imagining
I had tossed and turned
sleepless with guilt.

I wanted to tell you
neither one of us
was the victor,
but could only
stare past you.

You proceeded
to outline,
in great detail,
the more serious potentialities
of my child's illness.

I took the news
in my breaking heart,
cradling my broken baby,
and wished most ardently
you were still telling me
I was just
a foolish mother.

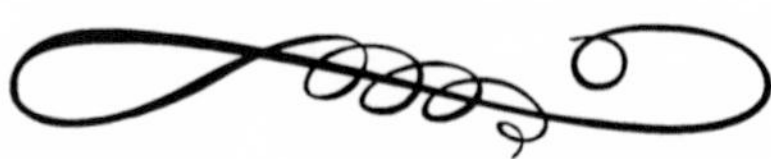

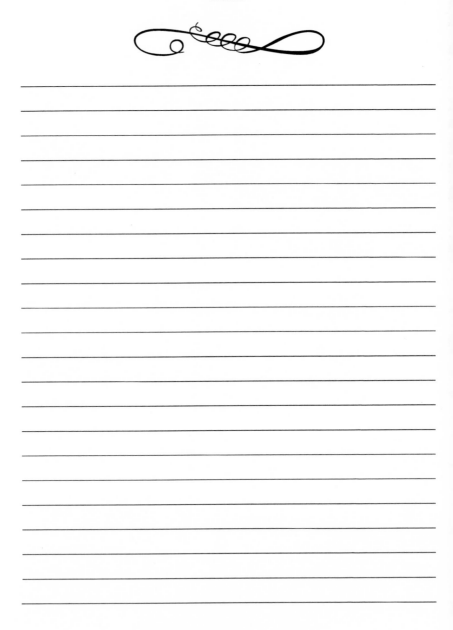

Mamamia

I never was one to panic.
I was assuring and calm,
having researched so many aspects of parenting,
I felt I could protect my babies.

But then came my changeling,
by her own design
she shaped the woman I am.
Her ills have rocked this mother's boat,
left me treading
in uncertain waters.

It is crushingly hard
to watch a wee one suffer so,
to choose for one who has no voice,
to never know
if what we do
will heal
or harm.

This is a heavy and constant weight
compressing my entire body.
My insides have felt so constricted,
my frame bent almost in two
by desperation's strength.

I have wanted to flee from this battle,
my head filled with shattered glass,
but something I cannot name
sucks the pieces back together
sending me again into the fire
to fiercely protect
my little one.

I must stand strong,
for it is my role alone

to question,
to look for truth in what the "experts" say,
to find answers,
accepting that for some things there will be no clarity,
no grand "Aha!"

I must bear the responsibility of choosing
when "They"
could take it all from me
if I'd follow
doctor's orders.

One doctor asked me why I was so bent
on researching all the pros and cons
of every treatment he'd suggest,
on understanding the details and history
of any case
similar to my daughter's.
Why not rest and leave that job to him?
Why not let him shoulder the burden
of making any possibly wrong
decisions?

I told him this would never do
for when we were through with all the guesswork
it would be me taking her home.
She was not his own,
not his lifelong commitment.

No, he could say he'd lost a few
while it may be true he's saving most,
but I have just this one to save.
And for my own preservation,
I must know that I do all I can,
that I think long, and hard,
and deep,
about every path we take.

For I am timelessly
bound to her
whatever the result
of our efforts.
And if some misjudge and feed my doubt,
I must stand my ground firmly,
knowing the sincerity
of my intent.

This is not a trial I can pass away
for through my womb she has come.
In my hands,
for now,
some part of her future rests.

So I must choose through wrong and right
how best to care for her,
searching tirelessly,
calling loudly,
for methods that will ease her way,
ease my way.

For I am her mother
dressed in armor
woven from threads
that hold together
the human heart in crisis.

Our lives are intertwined,
sweet and smooth,
sharp and pain filled.

She is my baby
wrapped in love and hope.
Connection is eternally ours.
We journey as one
to find the gift
in this twist

of fate.

We wander
in the veiled mists
of the mysterious,
where over and over,
we uncover life as our salvation
and learn to expect of it
no less
than the impossible.

Ordinary Divinity

Each dawn
I seek this cleansing place
a steaming cloth
upon my face
warm water
rushing over me
I drench myself
most rapturously

It's the only space
I am alone
inside my busy
child-filled home
so often
I will linger there
pretending
that I have no cares

My aches and sorrows
melt away
my strength returns
to greet the day
I sigh a stream
of well-soothed notes
through heaven's misty clouds
I float

And wander
where my mind may lead
to trips I'll take
to books I'll read
when someday soon
I have more time
to call my own
to call
all mine

For when I'm there
the clock slows down
most patiently
time waits around
for me
to be renewed
and clean
for me
to make my plans
and dream

Yes
each dawn
I seek this cleansing place
my visits there
I never waste
for liquid bliss
rains rich on me
sweet sips
of restful
reverie

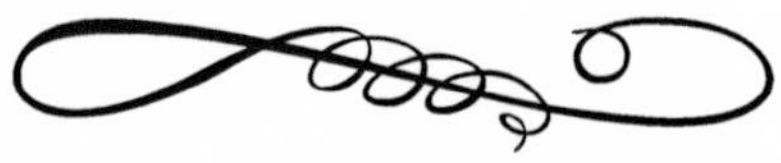

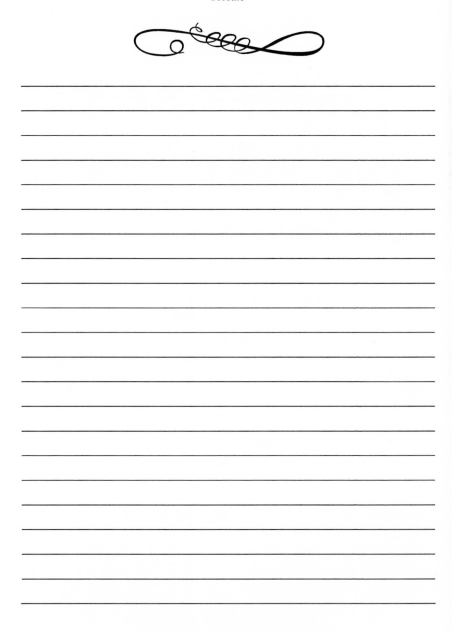

Kisses and Band-aids

I shatter,
splintered into a million pieces
by the news.
"Her brain is not developed."
I slump to the hospital floor.
She's only been tired,
a bit anemic.
Not this.
Run,
fast.
Regress.
Find somewhere safe.

A friend gently shakes me
with her words.
She knows where I want to go.
She's been there.
She gives me permission to go,
reminding me that I can stay awhile,
but not forever.
I know she is right.
She speaks from experience.
But still I go,
not ever wanting to return
to face my child
and her damaged brain.

My husband smoothes my hair,
touches my hands,
letting me know he'll cope,
telling me to rest.
And so I dive deeper,
so deep down
that I want kisses and band-aids.
I want my Mommy and Daddy.
I call for them.

Days later,
they come.
But I come back faster.

Now I do not need them
in the same way.
I am the parent again,
with my own band-aids and kisses
for my imperiled little girl,
my own ideas about what might be possible,
determined to make the broken whole,
to search out and put to the test all paths
that might mend her.

"Don't question them, listen to the doctors.
Why won't you listen to the doctors?"
My father puts his faith here
trusting in science.
"Look at yourself, you are skin and bones.
What right do you have to nurse this baby?
What right to question the doctors?"
My mother speaks in fear,
searching for the cause,
the blame.

I cannot listen to them.
I hear other voices
calling louder for my attention.
I shut out their worries,
sure that, right now, they have no
meaningful message for me.
We wander through a month
of shadowy, alarm filled minutes.
In and out of the emergency room,
setting up house again and again
in the too familiar hospital.
We seek healing,

but feel
only breaking.

Yet somehow, the storm quiets.
We are home.
Wreckage to wade through,
severed energy,
drained emotions,
disabled bodies,
searching minds.
It seems insurmountable at times.
Everyday pushes us
to the medical library,
a new doctor's office,
other parents,
books,
every place that might hold
an answer,
a cure,
a hope.

Our baby is slow.
She cannot move well.
No balance.
No smiles.
Her arm shakes in perpetual tremor.
We tell her sisters,
"Be careful with her.
Watch her head.
Don't let her fall.
Play with her on the ground.
Keep cushions around her.
Be careful."
We hover over her constantly
and worry.

And then one day,
while she is in the care of her father,

our middle daughter
wants to hold
her baby sister.

It has been so long.
She is so cute and helpless.
She takes her in her arms.
She lifts her up,
and up,
to see herself in the mirror.
But the baby slips out of her nine year old grasp
and falls,
falls,
falls,
head first to the hard wood floor.

I am in the kitchen.
They rush to me,
yelling my name.
I take my baby.
She is stunned.
She is bruised and bumped.
Panic overtakes me.
Has all our progress been destroyed?
Has she been set back again?
I cannot pick up these new pieces.
My fear becomes a weapon.

I scream accusingly,
"We told you not to pick her up!"
"Why weren't you watching her?"
I scream and scream,
an awful scene.
I give her up to my husband.
Someone else must make her better.
"Take her back to the hospital."
"GO!"

My sword-like tongue
lashes out at them,
leaving them badly wounded.

I collapse
in an ocean of tears,
lost in a typhonic rage of despair.
A wave of forceful proportions looms over me
and then it hits me.
This was your message to me,
Mom and Dad,
that the anguish seeks to quell itself
through anger and blame,
through handing over responsibility
in desperate hope
that there is some expert,
some god-like human,
who can make it all right.

I am flooded with compassion for us all.
I feel indebted for this lesson,
for I have been granted the opportunity
to stand in the shoes of my husband,
to stand in the shoes of my nine year old daughter.
And now I've walked in my parents' shoes too.
I know both sides intimately
and I grow.
I look past the fear,
and though not banishing it completely,
I've been given
the gift to see through it.

So in the end,
they did come to my rescue.
They soothed the soul of their child
by bringing me revelatory kisses and band-aids
more restorative,
more durable,

than any I had known before,
a curative wisdom that I can use,
in turn, to dissolve the scars
I have left on others.

And now, when I feel
the volcanic eruption of terror
begin to engulf me,
I am humbly confident
that it will not swallow me entirely,
it will not swallow my baby.
Still, it is not yet over,
this trip to hell.

But I am a new soldier,
supple enough to weather the fury,
fluid enough to quench the fire.
For in recognizing fear
as my sentry,
it has become my ally.

It hovers by my side
propelling me to rise over the battle,
lifting me up,
holding me up,
above the ruins.

And standing on top
of its mountainous shoulders of ash,
I can see further and more clearly
than I ever dreamt possible.
I can catch sight
of the promised land beyond,
knowing
that if I fall
there are always
kisses and band-aids.

Home

I lay wakeful
in the midnight
of hospital hush
and wish myself
to some other moment

how comforting
to just
be home

listening
to my oldest daughter
protest
yet another evening
of homework

I would smile
only reassurance
tonight

or refereeing
the ritual rows
of my two younger girls
over whose turn it is
who touched who
or some other
insurmountable
injustice

I would hear
only melodious voices
tonight

or preparing
the sixteen thousand
four hundred

and twenty-fifth
meal
of my motherhood decades
and washing
the two hundred forty-six thousand
one hundred
and ninety-fifth
dish

I would conduct
only symphonies
tonight

Or making the rounds
on tired legs
picking up toys
papers
clothes
and pausing
to read a story
calm fears
or indulge
in the retelling
of a day

I would dance
only pirouettes
tonight

or lying
as in these twenty years
in my own bed
just maybe
without
a little body
wedged
between his warmth
and mine

I would feel
only girlish fancies
tonight

how comforting
to just
be home

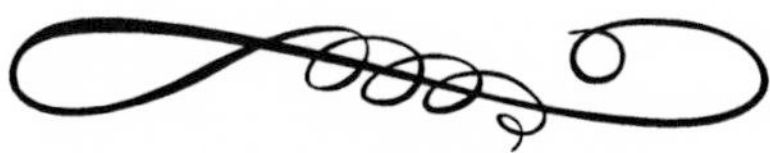

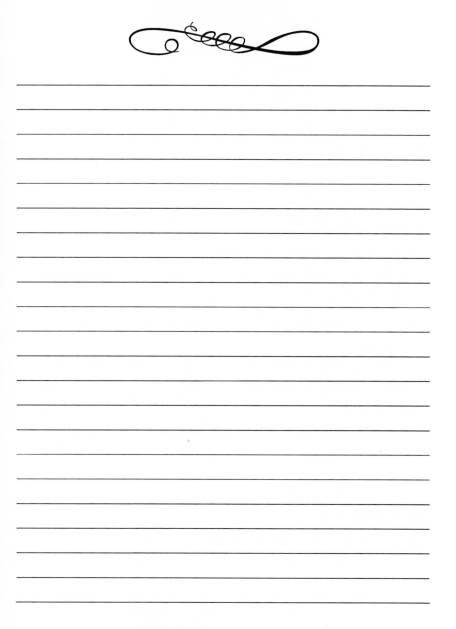

The Not Knowing

It is emotional torment
this not knowing
being on watch
waiting

Death lurks near
but it no longer terrifies
I have accepted that she will die
and be it now or later
I have already placed her
or rather
finally understood her place
in the hands
of the Infinite

It is not the pain of death
that crushes me so
it is the pain of living
the possibility
of a less than whole
mind
locked away
under the label
"abnormal"
eaten up
with injustice

The ghost of her future
haunts me with visions
bleak
yet very real
a life filled with restrictions
with "no"

Simple pleasures
small choices

grotesquely shadowed
with what ifs

The not knowing
is only the uncertainty
of when
certain terror
will strike

It is a place on the edge
a vast chasm below
perilous peaks all around
and I fear falling
in dark descent

And so I pound my body
into fatigue
that my mind may rest
terror be forgotten
that my shallow breath may deepen
waking me from this wicked dream
and that my strangled heart
may beat once more
with a ferocity
that reminds me
to live

On The Spectrum of Disorder

Come sweet angel of the night
let me close my eyes
drift inside
to deeply quiet places
let me sleep
undisturbed

Until
the ghostly threat
of foaming blue lips
in a white face
jerking limp limbs
on a deadweight body
and raspy
ancient breath
from smothered lungs
is gone
never to haunt me again

Until
the blank hollow
of absent eyes
frozen brain
is dissolved
into distant horror

Until
silence
vacant stare
random
repetitive mutterings
are replaced
with connected
communicative intent

Until

wandering back and forth
twirling and circling
up and down
are transformed
into purposeful movement

Until
laughter
surprise
disgust
poutiness
excitement
anger
curiosity
coyness
and compassion
replace stoic features
becoming expressions of meaningful abundance
worn at just the right time

Until
the now forbiddingly closed rooms
of wild imagination
shared play
open up their decorative doors
to welcome in my little one

I hold her tight
knowing she is a time bomb
capable of exploding us both
at any moment
deeper into the nightmare

Yet
even through this daily madness
hope finds me
giving me the courage

to champion
the small successes
the painful progressions
for even the most minute bit
of positive change
is bounteous
to my powerfully hungry heart

Still I long for sleep
that peaceful repose of the carefree
oh let me hibernate in innocent tranquility

Until
I reach the other side
where bodies are perfect
minds are whole
hearts are full
and spirits are knowing

I can talk up the blessings
of this testing ground
but the day-to-day living
of the uncertain present
the less certain future
lies beyond me

Constant supervision
a tornado of frustrations
explosive reactions
every bite of supposed nutrition
a potential assailant
familiar surroundings torn and peeling
everyday objects hurled like missiles
destruction

Serenity
protection
optimism

are lost to me
the world looms a dangerous place
and she is a danger
to herself

How can we control
the unknown
get a grip on this disease
understand how and why
it has manifested
in our small
defenseless baby

For she is on the spectrum of disorder
it has permeated all our lives
infesting every refuge of escape
forcing all to be out of place
chaotic

Her hours are minutely planned
her diet neurotically monitored
none of this
lots of that
ten therapists
twenty doctors
a hundred books
a thousand articles
a million worries
disordered order

And I just want to sleep
cradled in some slumbering dreamland
be kind
be still
and wake me only
when it is all over
all better
all right

Categorical Panoply

A categorical panoply
of vast and varied
therapies
to cure
or combat
ASD
all swim before my eyes!

And every claim
I've three times read
each mixed
and mingled
in my head
which one shall be
our daily bread
how am I to decide?

There's Melatonin
and SCD
Vitamins
and DMG
Hormones
Gluten/Casein free
and that just starts the list!

There's Feingold
Enzymes
Stimulants
Anti-psychotics
Oxidants
Prozac and other Happiants
such biochemic bliss!

There's Neurosensory
Integration
Proprioceptive

Stimulation
Facilitated
Communication
yet oh, indeed, there's more!

There's Therapeutic
Dance and Art
Hippotherapy
to start
Joint Compression
to impart
what else could be in store?

Social Stories
Modeling
Chairs to spin
and Chairs to swing
Psychomotor Patterning
and still so much to know!

Psycho-dynamics
ABA
Son-Rise has found
another way
PECS
and TEACCH
and Floortime play
each offer paths to go!

The options
all just pile up
they fill
and runneth o'er my cup
which shall I choose
to greedy sup
to reach my blessed babe?

For testimonies

rich abound
each method
has proponents found
and I am dizzy
all around
how will I find my way?

The Merry Band

The first week
in the hospital
I walked the halls
with my eyes closed
I did not want to see
more tear streaked faces
for sadness
I carried with me
everywhere
every moment

Yet
I could not
close my ears
and as I passed
I heard laughter

But how could they laugh
these parents
of a severely afflicted
permanently damaged
or heartbreakingly disabled
child

What did they find
to chuckle about
for I thought
I would never
smile again

By the fourth week
in the hospital
I had forced myself
to look
and even talk
with these parents

And I came to believe
that what appear
to be travesties
are often
answers
to our most fervent prayers

I had prayed for peace
for joy
and I got Mia

Through her
I have learned
to create my own light
to water a green shoot
in the barren earth
with the rain of my mirth
and nurture it
into some useful balm
for my wounded soul

We have no choice
we parents of the labeled ones
we must
form a merry band
or be crushed
by our sorrows

For because we feel pain
so often
so deeply
we must also learn
to feel delight
more often
more deeply

We simply must
learn to explode

bent over double
with laughter
snorts
giggles
lest we implode
with grief

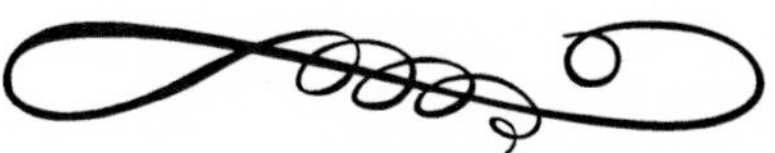

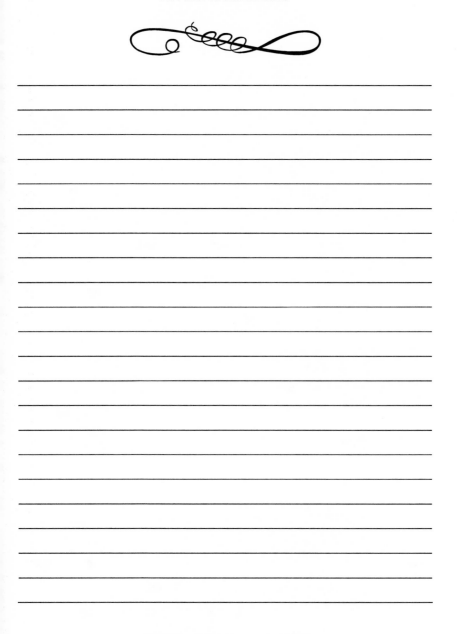

How Do I

How do I
stop you
for a moment
like the sun
stops the cold
slipping out
from under the clouds
to warm the earth
then
I will set you free
but you will have felt
love's touch

How do I
make you listen
like the seashells
listen for the waves
echoing the sea's music
in their own
enchanted voice
then
you may shut me out
but you will have heard
life's lullaby

How do I
make you see
like a prophet
sees man's destiny
unveiling the future
foretelling of glories
warning of despair
then
you may turn your head
but your eyes will be opened
to the mysterious

How do I
make you remember
like the seed
remembers the spring
pushing through darkness
toward the light
then
you can brave the winter
alone
but you will never forget
your way
home

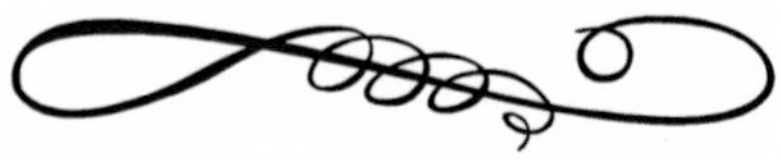

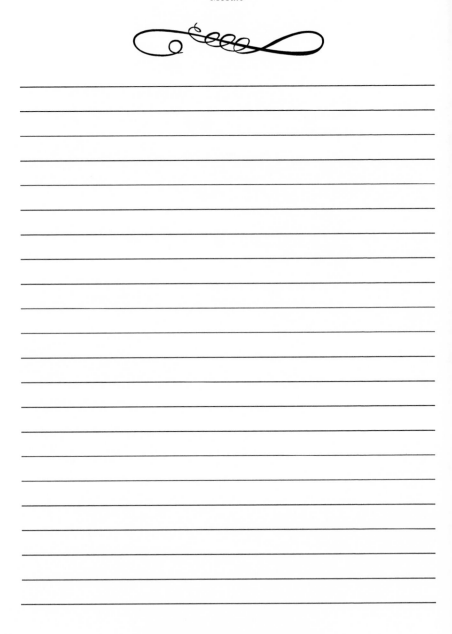

Enough

Stuck in my head
you are like a distant tune
not quite remembered
nor forgotten

You hover
in that in-between place
of the faintly understood
and I struggle
to bring you
to full consciousness

I catch myself
singing your verse
and wondering
with what softest kiss
you pressed your melody
to my lips

Oh
you are like a song
I have attempted to learn
so well
for so long
that I vacillate
between replay
and
enough already

Covering The Bases

Gluten Free/Casein Free for breakfast at seven

Kelly for Applied Behavior Analysis at eight

Melissa for Occupational Therapy at ten

Vera for Physical Therapy at eleven

Anna for Speech at noon

Specific Carbohydrate Diet for lunch at one

Ali for Floortime at two

Maretta for Sensory Integration Therapy at four

Vitamins for supplementation at five

Revised Specific Carbohydrate Diet for dinner at six

Diaper secured with pajamas on backwards for bed at seven

Nursery gates up and doors bolted for safety at eight

Review of additional therapies for consideration at nine

Mom for meltdown at ten

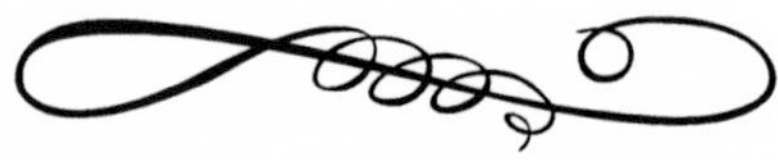

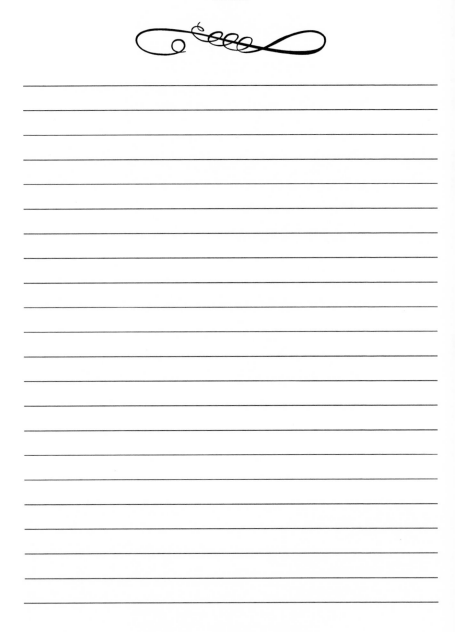

Hey, Little One

Hey, little one
where'd you go
you're lost in your mind
I know
I'd like to see what you see
but I long for you
here with me

This world may be
full of rules
of one-ways
of ridicule
but you've fallen
just like a star
and there's wonder
in who you are

How do we make
two worlds meet
touch ground
with such little feet
my tears fall
so hope can grow
I watch your eyes
come and go

You're veiled
in a distant haze
but sometimes
I catch your gaze
and I feel your sighs
long and deep
like whispers
in dream filled sleep

What gifts

do you bring this time
what water
changed into wine
what ribbons
wrap up your voice
what hands
mold this life of choice

The ups and downs never cease
a dance of catch
and release
you travel inside
alone
I ache
to give you a home

What gardener
grows flowers so thorned
to touch beauty
my flesh is torn
would I choose
less rose red blood
you've come
through this crimson flood

It's a struggle
through sacred places
the Holy
most troubled spaces
I fall
toward the wrath of fear
winged prayers
dull the sharpened spear

Will you ever tell
where you've been
open up

and let me in
would I hesitate
to pass through
would you pull me
along with you

We navigate separate ways
each turn
buried in this maze
but if you'll just
hold my hand
we'll bridge our paths
through this land

No certainty
lies ahead
bound together
this road
we'll tread

One smile
you fill my heart
one word
you lift the dark
reach out
give me something to believe
take love
I wait
ready to receive

Denial

Proud
having given up the lie
both great and small white
made falling
all the more
mortifying

Transformed
for a frozen moment
into some other
distortion
of myself

Kind words
a gentle angel's coo
creating cradled space
for correction
but receiving only
false testimony

Mechanical mouthings
foggy movements
and finally
the nauseating shock
at what my lips
had uttered

Through leagues of tears
I sunk deep
unearthing the burial ground
from whence
my traitorous words
arose

From this low place
I looked skyward

and understood
with desperate compassion
the weighty distance
of my fall

I had lived for a time
at the top
made strong by visions
of conquest
by communion with those
who had conquered
and conspiracy with those
determined yet
to prevail

But on coming down
from that heavenly height
to the expanse
of daily doing
I embraced anguish
and let it creep
masked as rational thought
into my soul

For when we have bathed
in that Holy water
on the mountain of glory
we come away perfumed
with the ripe scent
of the invincible
attracting the shadowy form
of doubt and fear
to tracks us
like a blood hound

And so it was
that some small scene

of the work
yet to be done
flung off handedly
in my face
pushed me soundlessly
into the void
and the only voice
I could recover
was that
of denial

Paths

The right way
universal
acceptable
powerful
has gone bust
like a balloon
inflated
with too much
hot air

The path
to recreating it
is darkened
obscured by vines
of disuse
disinterest

Yet all around me
lay sunlit roads
each suitable
for passage
each beckoning
to eager travelers

My task
is only to discern
which one
calls my name

And to stay alert
for the road signs
pointing me
once again
to turn
in another
direction

Part Two: Spoonfuls of Possibility

"For I know the plans I have for you, plans to prosper you and not to harm you, plans to give you hope and a future."

Jeremiah 29:11

You

You weigh only fifteen pounds
stand a fourth of my height
and yet
I am panicked
tottering with anxious anticipation

You scare me

All my years of mothering
through tears and tumbles
have not been preparation enough

You humble me

I am skittish
caring for you
unsure if my tendings
match your needs

You mystify me

You are distant
you do not respond readily
to my touch
my love

You spurn me

Still
I brave my fright
my confusion

Because
you came through me
made of my flesh
born of my blood

You chose me

And because
I feel it
even without your arms
reaching toward me

You save me

Interruption

My daughter's afternoon therapist
walked calmly
down the stairs
and said,
without alarm,
"I think
she may be having a seizure."

I startled
but then relaxed
for the first time
since these episodes
of apocalyptic terror
had begun.

Some soothing sedation
in Shuki's voice
stayed my usual panic.
Her assuring demeanor
caused me to pause
and think reasonably
about how
I wanted to proceed.

I recalled
that I had read,
some months ago,
about techniques
to successfully interrupt
epileptic patterns.

Looking thoughtfully at Mia,
just now beginning to drool,
her face turned
and eyes locked
fixedly to the left,

I wondered
what combination
of sound,
smell,
movement,
and sensation,
might break
her catatonic spell.

I took her from Shuki's arms
replaying every detail
of my constant observation,
suddenly inspired
to engage her mind
in familiar activities.

Setting her on bare feet,
gently coaxing
her stubborn head
toward midline,
I walked her outside.

Staring soft
into vacant gaze,
I sang favorite tunes,
handing her bits of rock,
flower,
twig,
and encouraging her
to hold them in her sight
for dazed examination.

She stumbled
like a novice drunk,
draining color,
saliva pouring thick and sappy
from limp blue lips.

Still, she heard me
across that vast
neurological divide
and after ten eternal minutes
she coughed,
vomited,
and began to whimper
for mama.

She had willed herself back
from the bridgeless brink,
heeding my call,
returning frightened,
confused,
and interminably exhausted
from her timeless journey.

Cradled in my embrace,
her feeble fingers
pulled wispily at her jaw
in repetitive succession,
until she drifted off,
hands stilling,
to restorative slumber.

My body melted
into relaxation
with her own,
smoothing tousled mane,
witnessing a rosy sunrise
of baby color
rise up warmly
in once ashen cheeks
and marveling,
stunned,
at the way of things.

What brought her back

I cannot say exactly,
perhaps
the feel of brick and pavement
on tender soles,
the sound of mother's voice
cooing well-loved verse,
the touch of prayer clasped hands
centering tiny face,
the sight of scavenged treasure
laid sacredly in trembling palm,
or the scent of summer air
mixed with sweaty determination.

But I can say
that no brief minutes
I have yet to live
have been so absent
of busy everyday worries
nor so filled
with impassioned,
consecrated,
communion.

Choose Again

It seemed the most important thing
you must be a thinker.

Your mind must be made to work
in ways both visible and audible.

This was the core of life,
what made it worth living.

If you could not be this,
it was better you not exist at all.

My fear.

And yet,
someplace in me understood,
everything has sacred purpose.

Your supposed deviations made me delve
more deeply still,
made words appear
channeled
in poetic verse.

Your existence
intensified the meaning
of all my actions,
allowing me to surface
through drowning pain,
to float unattached
past well-preserved scars,
dogmatic beliefs,
anticipated outcomes.

You are a chosen one,
in the company of many,

you show me the glory
of the uncertain,
the power of my vision
to shape past,
present,
future,
with eyes of my choosing.

I must do
what is paramount to me,
ponder
with relentlessness.

You must do
what is paramount to you,
challenge perspectives
with calamity.

For you
are my little angel of the dark,
whose light
is only hidden
from those
not yet ready
to see.

Possibility

She phoned me
on a shimmering
windblown summer noon
and warned me
to sit down.

She explained her review
of my daughter's chart
and her statistical findings
that 95% of all children
with such diminutive head size
are mentally retarded.

I thanked her for calling
and told her
I would collect a listing
of our family's cranial circumferences
and get back to her.

She said,
"WAIT,"
in a voice revealing
all the panic mine lacked
and confessed
she had been dreading this conversation,
afraid she would burst
my optimistic bubble.

I told her
I had no bubble
to be so thinly popped
though I appreciated her concern
and promised to be in the office
soon.

But as I hung up

it occurred to me
that what I did have
was a mountain
full of endless places to take refuge
and built ruggedly yielding
to withstand inclement weather.

And I knew then
there is no such thing
as false hope,
only true hope exists
and it keeps me rising
each dawn,
reaching
each day,
in a serendipitous storm
called
possibility.

Lessons

I will never forget
this exchange of words
on a dusk darkened day
traveling toward home
with the smallest of sages.

Slumped in the back seat
a disgruntled voice called out,
"I had a disgusting lesson today,
on bugs!
Who cares what all their body parts are called,
anyway?"

I considered my response
and the motherly moral
I intended to provide.
"I know what you mean.
I once had to do work on human parts,
learning all kinds of weird names
and examining microscopic sections
of human tissue.
It grossed me out sometimes too.
But you know,
when I was in the hospital with your sister,
I was glad to have had those lessons
so I could read and understand
all the medical reports."

"I'm really glad you learned that too, Mommy,
cause then,
if I have an autistic baby
when I grow up,
you can come and help me."

Caught off guard,
I earnestly stammered,

"Oh, honey,
I don't wish for you
to have a baby
with any problems."

Without skipping a beat
and in the most matter-of-fact tone,
she replied
"It will be okay, Mommy
as long as she's as cute
as Mia."

My voice was stilled,
emotions choked
on all my hoping
for more or different.

And I realized then
it was I
who held the misguided view.

For where I saw
dreaded dysfunction,
my little girl
saw only beauty.

And I vowed
that very day
to begin looking
with eight year old
eyes.

The Cloak You Wear

I watch you,
through the mirrored glass,
struggling to manipulate
the items placed before you,
to gain control
of your elusive
fine motor movements.

I look away
in pain,
your dysfunction
cutting deep
into my heart.

Why
is it so hard
to see you in this place,
my stomach rising to my throat,
pitching me
into vomitous revolt?

Here,
it is all laid out
in black and white,
the extent
of your "abnormalities,"
cloaking you so fully
I cannot recognize
the gifts you bring.

It is all about
what you cannot do
in these therapeutic rooms,
and some part of me
protests the picture
this scene paints of you.

I feel the blood of escape
running through my veins.

There must be a way
to serve you
without diminishing
the essence
of who you are.

I want to champion
the strength in you,
the intuitive instincts
you possess.

I want to honor
your pace and inclinations,
to know joy
in your presence.

I turn back.

Your eyes focus
in my direction.

I hear you whisper,
in wordless connection,
that I must look
beyond my sight,
for the cloak you wear
is one of my making
sewn with threads
of my fear.

And I know
only I
can change the garment
I have dressed you in.

I decide then,
enough,
time to tear off the rags
masquerading you
as hopelessly condemned,
and cast you instead
in the glorious role
of savior
rescuing me
from this play
of tortured acts.

Modifications

Old habits
have been modified
meeting pulse
and rush
of divergent stride

Our voices changed
no patterned tune
budding rise
feathered dip
like a roving moon

Watchful distance kept
from sudden claw
pinching grasp
lashing palm
that has struck us all

Our homes décor
has traded place
barren walls
tattered gut
and empty space

Tall furnishings
deranged
laid low
to squeeze the height
of falling blow

With crowning locks
our doors are maimed
to jail
or fortress
impulse
untamed

Over clovered lawn
and well-dressed wood
your nursery windows
nailed shut
for good

All weighty toys
kept far from use
only fur
sturdy cloth
weather your abuse

Cherished books
endangered
cautiously shared
pulling paws enamored
with paper
to tear

Family outings
fractioned
splintered in two
who dares
today
stand guard for you

Pajamas backwards
reengineered
to be zippered or buttoned
out of sight
in the rear
to forbid
picasso baby hands
the pungent paint
of soiled pants

All this

and more
with great thought
caring deems
to keep you
our dervish
out of harm
so it seems

And still
your smile broadens
at every turn
in triumphant acceptance
that we've finally learned
as if 'twas you
come here to teach
and take us
eyes opened
past tip-toed reach

Swat

In the grocery store,
I set you down momentarily
to pull a stubborn cart
from its nested bunch.

You run straight
into a pair
of bare legs
and begin assaulting
stationary thighs
with baby slaps
and painful pinches.

An irate face
jerks down,
eyes glaring with intolerance,
annoyed hands
swatting the air
surrounding you
as if you were
a more than pesky
fly.

I snatch you up
both horrified
at your actions
and astounded
by your victim's
response.

I place you in the seat
of our freed carriage
and pause to consider
confronting this battered woman,
defensively explaining
your lack of control

and indignantly demanding
an explanation
for her own.

But I pass on,
suddenly believing
the lesson was for me,
for how could I
ask her
to release
her shortsighted,
incriminating
judgment of you
and find compassion,
when I still stood,
paradoxically,
in reproachful judgment
of her.

Retreat

Sometimes
when you have uttered
the same word
for the hundredth time
flung
the millionth object
traced and retraced
the same circular path
I turn away

I retreat
to the indulgent luxury
of folding
the hundredth basket of laundry
washing
the millionth dish
sweeping
the same recently swept corners
along the ritualistic route
of my kitchen

These are tasks I know
with blind precision
their familiar rhythm
allows my mind to empty
sending me
into the meditative trance
of your world

I slumber deep
in this work
laboring almost without notice
and awake reminded
with great relief
what a calming refuge
you have chosen for yourself

Perceptions

I can choose
to look at your movements
with new eyes
casting aside the spectacles
of tragedy and loss,
replacing those dark glasses
with curious lenses
that allow my gaze
to be filtered
through appreciation and wonder.

From this view,
each gesture
is a valiant message,
illuminating all the dogmatic verse
you have come
to question.

And you sense my change,
the fear and expectation
dissolved,
heart opened
in hopeful acceptance.

I want much for you,
but am content,
intrigued,
to watch you
commune
in your way,
your time,
present to us both.

You bring a curative blessing
causing the "should" encrusted
scales of presumption

to fall away
from my sight.

For what are perceptions
but fistfuls
of fairy dust
we throw on our experiences
to paint them
the color of our beliefs.

Weary Feet

You routinely chance
harrowing heights,
one limb poised
at danger's door,
and I often dream
in waking moments
that you are suddenly
taken from me
by some accident of fate.

My feelings mix,
relief and anguish,
aware of your many needs,
how you hold captive
the pace of my days.

Without you,
I imagine
life might be
somehow easier
though decidedly
less revelational.

Your daily habits
are my delight
and my nightmare,
exuding both
intrigue
and repulsion.

But I have come to know
the choice is mine
to see pain
or joy
in your presence.
I intend

to choose
the lighter view,
yet I wander off
losing myself
in darkened places.

And it is always
my own awe
at your simple accomplishments,
the daring of your existence
that leads me back,
hopeful,
onto the sunlit path.

My insistence on walking
this crooked course
is testament
to my humanity
for in some way
each wobbly divergence
makes my gait steadier.

And whether sure or doubtful
each step traces lines
on a fickle map,
charted
by the mischievous offspring
of my beliefs,
who scatter
like windblown nymphs
and are born anew
in a continuous spiral
of discovery.

For the journey
toward you
is paved all along

with the tripping stones
of care and love,
it is dusty
with thick clouds
of acceptance
that unveil more
than they mask
and that I cannot help
but kick up
if my feet
are to march onward.

Worry-Free Child

I must look exhausted
to your little eyes
for you round up your sister
and entice her,
confidently,
up the stairs.

You bathe and pajama
her tiny frame
and she follows you
willingly
to her cozy bed,
fully spent
from concentrated hours
of daily therapy.

You tuck her in
amidst piles of books,
bring her water,
lay wakeful beside her
until her eyes close
heavy with sleep.

Slipping quietly
from the darkened room,
you beam with pride
having gently mothered
your precious sister.

You come to me,
curling up,
a contented kitten
in my lap.

My arms enfold you
with easy

familiarity.

Holding you
restores me,
warm softness
bathing my battled body
in healing touch.

The delirium
of your smell
perfumes the air
with fresh,
uncomplicated,
serenity.

I sink deep
in the cushion
of your breath,
gratified,
in no hurry
to move on.

You are wholly with me,
replacing the burdens
of my heart
with the weightless ecstasy
of your love.

Your small form
nestles effortlessly
in the mold
of my flesh,
releasing everything
to the peace
of this moment.

There is something

in you
that calms me,
something
I can trust
to grow strong.

Your future
is a finely woven net,
made strong
with history
it breaks
my fall.

You
are my comfort child,
smiling up at me
with faithful eyes,
you have not come
to test me.

Our joy in each other
is indescribably deep,
pulsing
through our joined hearts
like a well-fed
stream,
endless,
dependable,
worry-free.

Octopus Mom

I've got octopus arms
though I hide them all well,
I can juggle ten balls in the air,
I can clean, kiss, and feed
handling multiple needs
as I tend to my little ones' cares.

And it's truly quite grand
that I have twenty hands,
I'd be terrible slow
with just two.
They need food,
they need drinks,
bubbly baths,
and new shoes.
Where the day goes
I haven't a clue!

"Braid my hair."
"Spell this word."
"Make me feel better, please!"
They're depending on me
to know how.
"Sing a song."
"There's a bug!"
"Mom, she called me a name!"
And "I have to go pee
I mean now!"

"Gee, Mom
look at the squirrel!"
"Will you snuggle me close?"
"Is there really a God up above?"
And "Why won't she talk
or play like I do?"
"Will she learn how

before she grows up?"

"Moooom,
I've spilled and I'm wet!"
"How old is the earth?"
"Will you chase me
and roll down the hill?"
"Now I'm sad
and I'm hurt."
"It's a story I need."
"Read it twice,
Mommy, please say you will!"

Sure, I'm Octopus Mom
though I tire sometimes
and I drop a few balls
here and there.
Yet when chance takes me far
from the sound of their calls
I just worry I need to be there.

WHACK

I bring my face close,
leaning near you,
smiling into your tranquil eyes
and then,

"WHACK!"

Your unanticipated slap
rocks me,
not as much from hurt
as from disbelief.

Your expression is serene,
you have moved on,
the incident lingers only
in my mind.

My shock is always fresh
though I am no novice
to your beatings.

I take sensible precautions,
removing potential missiles,
pillowing my body,
matching my reflexes
to your own.

I routinely compress joints,
massage muscles,
apply the intense pressure
I imagine
you crave.

And I struggle
to decipher the significance
your violent eruptions

hold for you,
what compels you
to lash out
with no apparent anger
or discomfort.

I recall countless times
carrying you
snuggled against my chest,
your grateful head on my shoulder,
only to feel the searing pain
of sharp baby teeth
sunk deep in my flesh.

Or lying curled beside you,
encouraging you
toward gentle sleep,
lost in your angelic features
while suffering
the full weight
of carefully aimed limbs
flung hard across my head.

Such paradox
is commonplace
in this house.

I may be busily working
as you circle
not so far off
and feel the splitting savagery
of some handy object
hurled forcefully
at my body.

Or perhaps I am stroking
your soft skin,
your fine hair,

only to have tiny nails
bite long and bloody streaks
down my naked arms.

The element of surprise
is your greatest weapon,
you are quick
though never painless.

Yes, I know too well
the torrent of your impulse,
yet, I cannot name it devilry
for your look
remains that of some porcelain doll
forever molded into serenity.

And so
no matter the reality,
I have not come
to expect it of you.

I dwell on other images,
building a portrait of you
artfully composed
of the countless gifts
you have pounded
with brutal determination
upon my heart.

No, my little messenger,
I do not question your character
for shrouded in your Buddha-like state
you compel me to unmask life's blows
as loud reminders
of longed for revelations
waiting just below
my befuddled surface.

Your Cell

Your room
is painted lavender
with cloud like strokes
billowing beyond the walls
in puffs and tails
across your ceiling.

But the water-colored fish
floating inside a framed sea
and fanciful décor
of nursery mobiles
no longer adorn
your lullaby interior.

Your bed
boasts a spotless white duvet
sprouting a field of flowers
lying low and large,
a kingly cushion,
upon a creamy rugged floor.

But gone
are the two twin nightstands
and five drawered dresser
that once flanked
and faced
your cozy nest
serving as monkey perches
for your less than graceful antics.

Your door,
a solid sheet
of perfectly matched
purple hue,
has locks
scarring her front

and back
to keep you in.

Your windows
wide and tall
look out
over lawn and woods
where dogs,
squirrels,
birds,
and more,
frolic
before your mesmerized eyes.

But the gentle wind,
cooling night air,
never breathe their magic
beyond the securely shut,
nailed tight,
double-glass view,
of your beloved
outside.

Your closet is rich
with gay toys
and well-loved books,
but her doors are bolted
and her secrets revealed only
when you are guarded
from the destruction
you might sow
from her contents.

What a mockery you make
of simple things,
of the small delight
a lovingly furnished,
playfully stocked

child's chamber
might give.

My only choice
is to laugh
silently
along with you,
believing this web you weave
has its own purpose.

And so with great ceremony,
every morning,
I gleefully release you
and joyfully greet you
as you emerge
from your calculated cell.

Where Do They Go

I stood at the opened
refrigerator door
contemplating breakfast
when I heard your small voice
enunciate with shocking clarity,
"I want juice."

Startled by this first,
a full sentence
of three remarkably crafted words,
I hurried to honor
your fortuitous request
while applauding you
with enthusiastic praise,
"Nice asking! I love to hear your words!"

Later that same day
I offered you more juice
hungry to hear
those orchestral notes
once more.

But you could not
reach them
and despite your excitement
to consume my offering
you managed only
a slurred resemblance to "juice."

Where do they go,
those perfectly formed
intonations,
what black hole
swallows them
leaving your tongue
thick and clumsy?

Yours is a pattern
of speech
that ebbs and flows
as if you have installed
a regulatory dam
controlled
by some fickle gatekeeper.

Or perhaps
there is more purpose
in your auditory dance,
quickening and falling mute
to more fully seduce
my greedy ears,
ensuring you will always have
a captive audience
listening through the silence
with rapt attention
for the next
symphonic
movement.

Smooth and Jagged Treasure

I hear your sobs
before I hear your story,
and something in me
says,
"I know."

I find you
hiding under tangled hair
and shielding arms,
shoulders shaking
in unbearable grief.

You are mourning
the deeply felt loss
of comfort upended,
days sliced thin,
the two people you most depend upon
violently propelled
to some other dimension,
far from you.

The calm of home
invaded by tension,
a minefield of emotions
that even careful steps
cause to explode
in the blinding immediacy
of trauma.

The world outside
armed with disapproval,
as smiles and invitations to belong
are replaced with furrowed faces,
with suggestions that your irresponsible presence
and that of your ill-mannered sister
are not wanted,

not welcome.

You lament
these “unfair” assaults
on your once
secure life
and I am buried
beneath your sorrow.

How do I unearth the words
to soothe you,
to help you see
some chance at light
where darkness smothers
like a thick blanket of ash?

This is the moment
to cry with you,
so I do.

I tell you,
I too,
wish it wasn’t so.

And I pray,
I really pray,
for both of us.

Later,
you come to me
to say
you didn’t mean it,
you don’t really
hate your sister,
only what she steals
from your childhood,
what she demands

of my time.

Together
we solemnly acknowledge
what we have lost
and cover the wounds over,
bit by bit
with pieces
of what we have won.

We turn our tears
into covenant streams,
plunging unsure hands
into cold water
and searching with desperate eyes
for beauty.

We fish up smooth
and jagged treasure,
the fragments
her volcanic existence
has bequeathed us.

We hold each shard
close to our hearts
and lay them down slowly,
hopeful to make it a good way,
knowing that it is a long way
from shattered glass
to mosaic.

Those Who Went Before Me

I listened to Linda's story,
to Suzi's,
to Jen's,
and was inspired.

But also
overwhelmed,
intimidated,
small.

Can I do
what they have done?

I studied my heart,
envisioning my image
years from now.

What did I see?
What did I want to see?

Then I chose
a dash of Linda,
a sprinkling of Suzi,
a dollop of Jen.

Added time,
imperfection,
forgiveness.

Mixed in heaping spoonfuls
of possibility.

And began to cook up
my own
story.

Part Three: Breathing Deep

"Arise, shine, for your light has come . . ."

Isaiah 60:1

The Bridge

You are strong
when I am crumbling bone
carrying me

I rise
when you are crashing timber
catching you

We stand
and take each blow
alternately
hurting for the other
for ourselves
our baby

You speak
when my voice
is swallowed
in misery's mire

I decide
when your thoughts
fly wild
in tornadoed tumble

We each
step up
to the plate
emerging from our pain
helmeted and swinging
seldom missing
our turn
at bat

But occasionally
both

sitting out
on the same bench
weeping tears
alone in our pain
head to shoulder

We draw and lose strength
knowing
this crisis
this illness
can create
uncrossable divides
or build
merciful bridges

Often
we look longingly
at the divide
imaging the lightness
of unleashing our burdens
into its depths

Yet
we remain
tethered
by threads of hope
to the bridge
where we hold tight
as it creaks
and groans
with the weight of us

Little Muse

I love
that you are my fourth
baby girl
causing me to reexamine
all that I am
by boldly interrupting
my careful plans

Insisting that I hear you
even from the womb
sending messages
to clear misconceptions
with dramatic flair

Forcing me to face
and overcome
my fears
by reconciling me
with distant worlds

Guiding me
to seek help for you
from people with dynamically
opposing views
with the understanding that ultimately
life is never
about "us versus them"

Opening me
to finding meaning
in pain
by tossing me
heart first
into excruciating fires

Wiping away

all traces
of righteousness
through elusive cures
and extensive controversy
over the existence of any sure answers
to your mystifying symptoms

Pushing me
to find balance
in my life
in the lives of those I shepherd
as you unwaveringly quest
to scale the most impossible of heights
throwing physical prowess
into the face
of your once shaky
uncertain
beginnings

And leading me
to measure each person's progress
against their own pace alone
as you confidently
refuse
to conform
to the "norm"

But most of all I love
that you taught me
to crave laughter
by your temporary inability
to express even the slightest bit
of joy
and now
as you giggle
with such total and infectious glee
I promise

smallest muse
as the drama of our lives together unfolds
I shall always
look for the opportunity
to roar
in delicious hilarity
with all
my little women

On The Mountain

We went to the mountain
hand in hand,
man and woman,
clothed in our sorrows
and were told
we could smile again,
stop pitying you,
and realize
you were not crying to be saved,
only we cried for salvation.

So we dried our tears
and it was good.

We were told we could recast tragedy,
find humor
in your routinely ridiculous rituals,
play a clown for you
in wonderfully wacky ways.

So we laughed
and it was good.

We were told that, after all,
fortune and disaster
are just different points of the same view
and we could decide that very day
you were our greatest gift.

So we saw our bounty
and it was good.

We were told we could believe
you were doing
the best you could,
taking care of yourself

by slipping behind protective barriers,
swaying meditatively
in your healing dance.

So we marveled at you
and it was good.

We were told we could join you
in your solitary world,
connect
through an accepting love,
wait patiently for you
to acknowledge us.

So we played by your side
and it was good.

We were told we could bury our burdens
in the soil of hope
and from those seeds
grow a garden of plenty.

So we prepared for the harvest
and it was good.

Yes, we went to the mountain
and were told
we could chisel
permissive words
on the tablet of our souls,
release our fear
to choose happiness.

So we did
and it is heaven.

Just Say Yes

"Just tell her no!"
"Discipline that child!"
"Don't let her get away with that!"
"Stop her!"

white noise
background
static
she doesn't register these cries for correction
she has no natural instinct to be socially acceptable
the concept simply doesn't exist
for her

she does not consciously
dwell on us

slaps
angry words
and physical manipulation
would only drive her more deeply inward
seeking escape from external stimuli
that she does not connect with
or understand

she withers
under forced conformity
and i wither
watching these so-called
therapeutic means

there must be another way

if she cannot enter into my custom of habit
perhaps i can enter into hers
perhaps in joining her chosen activities
mimicking her behaviors

we will discover
each other

she walks in circles
tapping together two objects
like size
shape
weight
a rhythmic beat
i follow her lead
trailing in unison

she glances sidelong
briefly
seeming to take me in for the first time
appraising my skill
i am doing something she knows
new possibilities open to us both

i immerse myself in her repetitious activities
becoming as adept as she

lining up objects with calibrated precision

chanting monosyllabic incantations

staring fixedly at minute details

marching in patterned circles

or swinging my head upside down
as the breeze i create billows through my hair

by creating space for her inclinations
i have found a meaningful way
to be with her
to study purposefully
what she does

delight in her intrigues

the habits i was so earnestly urged
to annihilate
become my roadmap
to reach her

and as we throw
bang
climb
twirl
i experiment with useful twists

she pounds on me
the wall
i grab a drum
offer her one as well
beating it with excitement
exaggerated pleasure
saying
"Oh you want to hit, drums are for hitting!"

she throws a toy in my direction
i grab a ball for each of us
"Throwing is great!
Balls are for throwing!
People are for throwing balls with!"

she begins to copy my actions
and over time
she accepts these gentle
enthusiastic suggestions
into her repertoire
of preferred behaviors
slowly
gracefully
making the transition

now she sees me
hears me
feels me

the disapproval
the preferences of others
still do not
quite
impress her

yet acknowledgement
encouragement
have gained me
selective entrance
into her fascinating world
and have pushed the door
a crack open
leading her
toward mine

Wise Women

Leaving,
once again,
the chilling office
of, yet another,
specialist,
I am frozen
in the icy sleep
of prognosis,
bleak assessment,
pragmatic foreboding.

I shiver myself awake
remembering
that this doctor
has no fuller means
of assessing my dear one
for neither time
nor tools
allow him to move beyond
the limiting task
of tragic diagnosis.

His programmed glimpse
shows only
a child who does not respond
"appropriately"
to his formula testing
and must, therefore,
be labeled
"wanting."

I wish for him
better lenses
and turn my thoughts
most gladly
toward the circle

of wise women
gathered
around my hearth
who through countless hours
and soulful touch
deeply
know my child.

Their knowing
reaches beyond surface realism,
beyond scientific calibration,
lodging itself,
instead,
firmly
in the intuitive
day to day
of familiarity,
forging bonds
that hold tight
through trauma
and triumph.

Here
my little girl
is the center
of a celestial web.

Together
we spin strong,
far reaching threads,
and weave connections
of talent
and promise.

In this shimmering cocoon
of warm arms,
ready smiles,

and conspiratorial hopes,
my daughter
is more truly measured
by keener eyes.

She is crowned
magnificent.

And my heart
is thawed.

Crazy

You make a mess
wherever you go.

You grab,
break,
bite,
throw.

It's a phase you're in,
wielding destruction
like crazy.

Tossing your food
all over the floor,
you just keep
asking for more,
with an edible grin.

Grabbing handfuls
like crazy.

You climb high,
fall on your face,
cut your lip,
your little knees scrape.

You just do it again,
taking chances
like crazy.

And when you stumble,
I rush to your side,
fill with panic
at the sound of your cry.

I see everything spin,

feeling worried
like crazy.

But then you giggle,
hug me real tight,
melt my heart,
turn fear to delight.

I get carried away,
cause I love you
like crazy.

The Sensation of Things

You love the sensation of things
in a way
I have never
witnessed them loved.

To you,
a bar of soap
is an irresistible delight,
the slippery feel
of its body,
the sudsy taste
of its bubbles,
make you smile wide
with irrepressible satisfaction
as if you have found a treasure
no other being
has ever justly known
how to enjoy.

The sight of food
throws you into frantic desire,
and it is not just physical hunger
igniting you
to such lust,
but some greater emotional craving
for with desperate intensity
you insist
on carrying packages
of bite-sized provisions
in your baby clutches,
fingering them sacredly,
like the smallest
of bag ladies.

You are passionately enamored
with the vast

and permissible outdoors,
wandering in meditative splendor,
you explore nature's spaces
in triumphant abandon,
and when you cannot be there,
you stare mesmerized
out any window
as if you have willed
a part of yourself
through the glass
with your longing.

Sudden force intrigues you
to the point of outrageous obsession,
you propel,
without tire,
object upon object
just for the joy
of letting it fly,
you thrust
with quick slaps
at any target within your reach,
and with placid gaze
you seem to digest
the repercussive vibrations
as necessary nourishment.

Strobotic dance defines your rhythm,
your pace is constant,
exhaustive,
up and down,
side to side,
circling round,
every task unfinished
but not forgotten
as if you know
there is so much
from which to choose

and are determined to frenetically sample
and eventually devour
every pie.

At dusk,
when the bell tolls your hour,
I lay your blonde,
mussy head
upon a pillow,
and with great relief
kiss your puckering lips
goodnight.

I slip beyond your door,
breathing deep on the other side,
filling my lungs
with all the space
you take up
by day.

These dark hours are mine
and I live well in them
knowing you drift to sleep
in contentment
for you do not contemplate the future
or toil
with what ifs.

Your focus
is the moment
and every one
is spent
in sweet and utter
blissful
sensation.

Wild Thing

You are a wild thing
and the possibilities of our woods
mix with your blood
like kin.

You are swallowed in them
without ever losing your way
for your path is not to tame
nor be tamed.

You claim each step
with confidence,
allowing vined and rooted floor
to wipe away
the trace of your trail
in a constant game
of checkmate,
requiring calculated thought
from neither you
nor nature.

You shuffle
through fallen debris,
paw
at muck and hollowed tree
as if these
were your truest toys.

Your child's games
are solitary investigations
of all that can be scooped,
dug,
dislodged,
peeled,
tasted,
and thrown.

You commune
with this arborous sanctuary
in total acceptance,
nothing forbidden or amiss.

Here thrives a mecca of treasure
laid bare
and your busy hands
leave no sacred gift
unexplored.

You are welcomed
by Eden's twin
as in no other place.

This tangled corner throbs
in gratitude
for the attention you lavish on her,
rediscovering her own beauty
through the looking glass
of your eyes.

Your pulses
mate in a dance
of revelational moments,
no beat to keep,
no rhythm to define you.

This is freedom at its finest,
your unmarked soul
inhaling lush unbridled visions
with innocent desire,
fingering lusty bounty
with permissible want.

I watch from afar,
hesitant
to call to you,

not wishing to halt
the holiness
of your trance.

I send my summons
like a whisper,
windswept
from my lips,
an echoing breeze.

In time,
you feel my presence
circling round you
in gentle flight.

You turn your rosied face
and will yourself
back to me.

You do not begrudge me
this interruption.

Some things you know,
even when you appear
to be absent
and have no words
to tell me.

Your coming
reminds me of this,
assuring me
that our connection,
too,
is sanctified,
of another
world.

Compassion

Yesterday,
waist deep in the baby pool,
you mended a piece of my heart
with one momentary gesture.

I whooped
and congratulated you,
fussing much over this act,
and calling over
your sisters
and father
to hear the news.

A mother
sitting nearby,
who had also witnessed the scene,
looked perplexed at my elation,
after all,
you had only comforted a crying child,
younger than yourself,
by offering him the toy
you were playing with.

But what could she understand
of your years of indifference
to the pain of others,
of your penchant
for sudden violence.

I only smiled
in return to her questioning glance,
proud beyond her knowing
to count my daughter,
at last,
among the compassionate.

Stepping Into Your World

In our world
you were frowned upon
by passersby
with tut-tuts and sadly shaking heads,
labeled deviant
by diligent doctors
conducting norm conforming tests,
wept over
by parents
whose dashed hopes crashed relentlessly
against your stony gaze.
In our world
you were caged
by "NO!"

But through tear-washed eyes
we saw the myths imprisoning you
and gathering up the fragments of our dreams
we built of them a wonderland,
a place peopled with your kind
a world that would free you
by "Yes."

And the miracle is we were freed too,
for in this room of magic
we mirrored your actions,
became your truer kin,
and found that your path was greater
than any we might have laid out for you.

We started with bare walls
painted soft yellow,
hung with high shelves and hooks
to display a dreamland of toys and books
tempting you to chance
syllables of request

enlisting our help to retrieve an object of your desire.
We laid out a soft rug to cradle tantruming falls,
to cushion hands and knees in rollicking play,
scattered pillows and blankets
to construct dim-lit hideouts and cozy reading nooks,
or to hug tight to our bodies against random baby blows.

We set up a heavy wooden trundle frame
reversed to serve as weighty and low table,
perfect for coloring, working puzzles, eating meals
and secure against a sudden impulse to upend.

In the door of your palace,
we cut a mirrored window
beyond which a darkened room gives cover
for silent observation
of camera and crew
intent on understanding
how best to play with you,
to engage with you
in mutually motivational learning.

These are but the fittings of a place
designed to reach you,
the trappings of a room made heaven
not by its contents
but by the thoughtful intent
skillfully woven
into every element.

Here we know connection to be a sacred gift,
we hold it out to you with loving hands
and receive it from you with full hearts.
We join you enthusiastically
letting you be the teacher,
knowing our role to be that of student
surpassing the teacher
only to inspire us both

to greater heights.

We nurture our relationship with you
by being genuinely grateful
for the ideas and feelings you share with us
for at one time your range of activities was so narrow,
your ability to emote
nonexistent.

We do not demand "appropriate" behavior from you
but rather model useful behavior for you
with uproarious antics that propel you
to joyfully copy our ways.

We demonstrate social interaction for you,
greetings, turn taking, play skills,
we share enthusiastically,
"yes, please have this toy."
you learn what you see,
what you feel,
from us.

We teach you games,
imagination,
attention span
by delighting in these things ourselves.
We display a broad range of emotions,
pointing out each one in exaggerated fashion.
We animate a toy to role play answering questions,
engaging in conversation, playing nice, learning new skills.

We talk to you about the names of things
and how they are best used,
sharing ourselves, our interests, our joys and sorrows
with wide-eyed wonder,
we offer you our knowledge of the world,
its mechanics,

its educational and communal customs.

We help you transition smoothly
from one activity to the next
by creating bridges you can understand,
by enjoying the movement ourselves.

We let loose in your playroom,
finding the outrageously imaginative part of ourselves.
We are warm, interested, energized, goofy, fun-loving.
We have a great time with our theatrics,
are entertained and entertaining,
reinventing ourselves over and over
to be the best toy in the room.

When you lash out,
we say gently,
"I like to be touched nicely, like this.
I am going to visit my friends in the corner
who touch gently.
Come over if you want to touch nicely with us."
We show you how we want to be treated
and invite you to join us in loving interaction.

We let go of expectations
when we step into your room
allowing you to choose us or not.
We do not judge our time with you based on your responses
but only on our ability to be open-hearted,
observant,
present.

We use positive language
to tell you what you can do
rather than what you can not.
We say, "Crayons are for writing on paper,"
"Walls are for holding up the house."
We are wacky

and demonstrative
with our explanations
allowing you to accept them gracefully.

We jump on opportunities to communicate.
When you speak we listen,
when you ask for something we respond,
telling you how happy we are to get it for you,
working with you to use a fuller sentence,
helping you get the most out of your speech,
introducing new ideas,
enunciating clearly.

When you can not reach your words,
we give them to you,
slowly,
allowing you time
to form them on your own tongue,
rooting for you,
championing your effort.

We are your biggest fans,
cheering every attempt at language,
interactive play,
or kind social gesture.
We shout our praise,
sing our congratulations,
applaud, dance, or sincerely whisper
our appreciation.

We make the world a friendly place.
We are easy to let in.
We give you our deepest respect,
honor your inclinations with reverence,
and you pick this up
more clearly than any discipline
of word or hand

Simple Joys

A laugh
when we've shared
something funny
words
from the heart
"I love you, Mommy"
a lingering glance
eyes focused
clear
sweet recognition
when we are near

Such simple joys
I finally know
our spectrum beast
no longer foe

And with throaty growl
you're a monstrous cat
pretending this
imagining that
a world of "yes"
doors opened wide
we coaxed our fears
to step aside

No painful sounds
or covered ears
no bolted doors
or hopeless tears
your opened eyes
dance light
amused
your mind's awake
to learn
and choose

We built our bridge
to face this ghost
hard now to say
who traveled most
one world or two
our choice to be
bound or adorned
by our “dis-ease”

Just Keep Seeking

Often,
a heartbreaking struggle,
our adorable eight year old
bumped through years
of considerably less
than cute
behaviors.

Phases of total absence,
a shell of a child,
terrifying seizures,
appearing to be
in the throes of death,
aggression,
mute insistence,
taking a great toll
on our patience,
our peace.

Dietary shuffles,
detailed recipes and protocol
amassed by dedicated parents
to salvage the guts
of our young,
suspected allergies,
reactive rashes,
food roulette.

Game for every method,
we rotated through
numerous therapies,
each with a beneficial effect,
though none so great
as the simple shift in perspective
that vanquished our distress,
allowing us

to see her correctness
and appreciate
her able methods
of coping.

Prayers and chants,
a circle of faiths,
gathered round her
in united concurrence
that Thy will be done,
yet hopeful
to inspire that will
toward matching our own
in grateful healing.

Heaven heard,
spilling luminous light
and loving hands
upon us,
sending gifted angels,
masked as ordinary
men and women,
to stroke our daughter's soul
with gentle communion.

We filled her so completely
that her heart burst open
to connection,
and we,
the parched abandoned,
inebriated ourselves
in the blessed waters
of her words and gestures,
splashed in our direction
through purposeful eyes.

It is a long river

and we have far to paddle,
but we no longer dread
the rapids and falls
for she is well on her way
in the journey of a lifetime.

Together we row our boat
down this stream merrily
and the tune we sing
is rich with hope,
"just keep seeking,
just keep seeking,
and ye shall find."

Even Now

Even now there are moments
when my blanket decision
to choose happiness
frays at the edges,
the threads unravel
leaving me with haunting questions
ravenous longing.

I want to hold her tightly,
will a fluid tongue,
a scholar's wit,
a philosopher's ponderings,
into her very being.

Oh, I want much for this child.

My wanting propels me
to scrutinize every nuance
of her movements,
her speech,
her comprehension.

Hours spent just watching,
wondering,
planning,
around this little one,
for I seek
the charmed reward
of profound conversation
with one who sparkles
just beyond reach.

Yet, even as I finger those loosened strings,
I deftly weave them back into place,
quiet in the presence
of her humble language,

transmitting heart to heart,
and as always
I decide
to understand.

For it is indeed possible
to deeply know,
to deeply love,
that for which we have never had
a single shred of sensory proof
for it is only belief
that makes a thing so.

And when I tuck the quilted comfort
of my contentment
around the two of us,
burrow warm
into its feathered folds,
I can lay my head
upon the pillow of my dreaming
and sleep peacefully
in all
that is
as it should be.

Something More than Happiness

He is screaming,
hitting,
pulling his mother's hair,
determined to be let out,
banging at the closed door.

His mother's face falls,
misery grabbing at her heart,
coloring her child's actions
with warning signs
of dreaded unhappiness.

So she opens the door,
releasing him from connection,
freeing him to wander,
circling,
smiling,
content.

We walk from the room,
tailing him.
She struggles
to breathe easier.

"That was hard for you?" I offer.
She nods.

"Why?"

"He is normally so peaceful."

"What is it you want for your child?"

"Happiness," she says.

"Do you think he is happy now?"

She glances at him
moving though space with fleeting awareness,
"Yes."

"Then why run a therapy program?"

She looks at me
surprised,
even appalled.

"What do you really want?" I inquire softly
as much to her as to myself.

"I want to connect with my son,
talk with him,
hear him communicate,
watch him grow,
witness his blossoming
into this communal
world."

I spin back,
lost
in my own recognition of her words
recalling myself
living
where she dwells now.

"Yes," I sigh,
humbled that she has found words for it,
"that is what I want too.
I want something more
for and from
my daughter
because I desire to know her,
to offer her the beauty
of social connection.
It is most truly about

what I wish
for myself.
And now that I am clear
on that
I guess it really is
okay."

She takes in my words
with a look I understand,
a look that means,
"I am trying to take this all in,
make it mine,
see
if it fits."

Tears fill her eyes
and mine,
for we know
that what we most truly hope for
is not some monotonous state
of permanent contentment,
but the thrilling,
lusty life
of deep
rollercoaster
emotions.

And ultimately,
the defining waves
of fulfillment
crashing mightily
on the sandy grains
of effort,
accomplishment,
and failure.

For it is these things,

together,
that make up the shore
of meaningful
play,
work,
love.

No,
happiness is not the word
to describe our dreams.

What we seek
has no name
but is rather a host of adjectives
to describe a life well lived,
a life consummated by that secret smile,
too big for the lips
yet held infinitely in the eyes
staring back from the glass.

Can This Be True?

Can this be true?

It is almost too much to believe,
these seemingly sudden turns.
She has changed her pattern
of being so unexpectedly,
that I have yet to change
my own habit of mind.

She speaks to us in sentences,
words of pure music,
sounding strong and clear
like the bugle of a rescuing cavalry
liberating our giddy ears!

She's moved from repetitive nouns and verbs
to pronouns, prepositions,
articles, and adjectives,
which pepper her melodic phrases
with a scent we inhale like air itself!

She asks for hugs and kisses,
and gives them often
with smiles and giggles
and baby arms wrapped tightly
around our overwhelmed shoulders!

She laughs uproariously
when we ham it up
and finds her own antics
just as entertaining!

Well past seconds now,
she spends long sweet minutes,
even hours
engrossed in interactive games

with eager playmates.
She even imagines monsters growling,
owls calling,
and toys greeting her!

Such normal,
everyday stunts
for any young child,
but for our child these things
are mountains of accomplishment!

They are hard earned trophies
she presses into our hands,
inflating our hopes,
filling our hearts,
enlarging our lives!

Can this be true?

For ours is a child who once protected her delicate senses
by covering her ears from unknown sounds,
humming to block out requests,
sliding out of chairs to avoid looking at a puzzle,
walking in circles to create a meditative dance,
climbing high to feel balanced and weighted,
throwing,
pulling,
biting to fill sensory needs,
and shunning interactive play
to avoid sensory overload.

This same child
now clamors for attention,
delights in the sounds and sights that surround her,
mimics our words and intonations,
invites us to hold her lovingly,
to be with her

in imaginative,
playful ways!

The fog has lifted from her world,
yet my head is still full of clouded memories,
silver lined to be sure,
for she has chosen to come to us
as we chose to go to her!

And her coming
is an event of such magnitude
that I imagine I will spend years ahead
absorbing and drinking in
the fragile wonder of it all!

Silk and Thorns

Her eyes how they sparkle,
her countenance how merry.
Her cheeks when she's flushed
are as red as two cherries.
Her lashes are long,
her feet never tire.
She moves like a gust,
spiraling higher and higher,
and the hair on her head
is all sunshine and curl.
It's hard to imagine
a more beautiful girl.

Her lips when they curl
form a smile that just dazzles,
while her antics and capers
make her dear family frazzle.
She can giggle and cackle
with hilarious glee
and in short
she's as nuts as a baby can be.
But her joy is all real,
and it's hard to be callous,
she may kick out and slap
but her heart bears no malice.

She's a jolly young imp,
all movement and chatter,
and she's caused us to dwell
on the things that most matter,
for her miniature tongue
can now run at great speed
and repeat without mercy
that she's desperate to feed,
or perhaps it's the course of the day
she's repeating,

she will babble until
our poor heads take a beating.
Still, this gift of her speech
we work hard to recall,
for there once was a time
when she spoke not at all.

Oh, she has a few flaws
and we all duly know it.
If an object is near to her grasp,
she may throw it,
for it's pressure she craves,
her taxed brain overloading.
We have all felt the force
of our Mia exploding.
Her senses are raw,
her skull ever tender.
Still, with all we've been through,
we are quick to remember,
we prefer her full conscious
and causing a fuss
then seizing,
and scaring the sense out of us.

And her entrance in school's
an incredible feat.
Every morning by eight
she is taking her leave.
How they keep her in check
is just anyone's guess,
but she's learning and pleased,
and I have to confess
that my days are quite changed,
I am feeling more rested
for the tears and the sweat
we with gusto invested
like a prayer to the heavens

on light wings through the sky
whispered hope in a God
who'd not idle nearby,
but would hark to our plea
with a wave of his hand
sending angels of light
to save His lost lambs.

For each heartache, each trial
each hope, and each sigh
like a thirst quenching rain
when the land has been dry
caused a small seed to sprout
to uncurl sturdy vines
growing sure towards the sun
and in nature's good time
bursting forth such a rose
in whose bloom none can mourn
soothed by petals of silk
and well taught by her thorns.

Hush

I remain
so utterly fallible
spending entire days
in the valley of tears
draining my doubts
emptying space

God has wrought miracles
before my sight
yet I see the broken road ahead
and despair

My power alone
is insufficient
this I know

Yet when I wander
in the desert of my want
I forget
that I need not
go it alone

Until by grace
my cries hush
to the voice of the Spirit
sending me door to door
to drink in comfort
compassion
friendship

And reminding me
to lift my eyes skyward
so I can fill up
once more
on faith

May your roots go down deep in the soil
of God's marvelous love."

Ephesians 3:17

About the Author

Elizabeth began working on the pieces in *Mosaic* in July 2001, shortly after her youngest daughter, Mia, was hospitalized. These writings were an attempt to hold onto some semblance of sanity and gain perspective at a time when nothing seemed to make sense. Elizabeth was shattered by her daughter's diagnosis of autism and epilepsy. She began writing, desperate to find some silver lining in this ominous cloud, as a means to think it all through. She shared her stories with other mothers experiencing the same trauma and was urged to compile all the work and publish this book. And so, *Mosaic* was born, representing the feeling so many share as they journey with autism, while also being Elizabeth's stone of remembrance for all the howling, doubt, pleading, and thanksgiving she issued up to the heavens, as well as all the miracles, patience, strength, and perspective she received back from our gracious God.

Originally from Iowa, surrounded by rolling farmlands and expansive sky, Elizabeth spent the majority of her adult life on the East Coast, ranging as far north as Quebec and as far south as Florida. She currently lives in Georgia with her husband of 23 years and their four daughters. Here, she works with parents and organizations to provide greater educational and emotional support for all families affected by an autism diagnosis. A portion of all proceeds from *Mosaic* supports educational programs for children and families.

To contact the author or purchase copies of *Mosaic,* please visit

www.livingthemosaic.com

Autism Website Resources

Autism Society of America: Fundraising, Awareness, Education
www.asa.org

Autism Speaks: Fundraising, Research, Education and Awareness
www.autismspeaks.org

Autism Treatment Center of America: Therapeutic Intervention
www.autismtreatmentcenter.org

Believe In Me Foundation: Fundraising and Education
www.believeinme.com

Breaking the Vicious Cycle: Specific Carbohydrate Dietary Intervention
www.breakingtheviciouscycle.org

Dr. Greenspan's Floortime Therapy: Therapeutic Intervention
www.floortime.org

Dr. John Hick's Pathways Medical Advocates
www.pathwaysmed.com

HANDLE: Gentle Neurosensory Enhancement Techniques
www.handle.org

Jacob's Ladder: Therapeutic Intervention
www.jacobsladdercenter.com

Kyle's Treehouse: Information and Support
www.kylestreehouse.org

Living The Mosaic: Information and Support
www.livingthemosaic.com

Lovaas Applied Behavior Analysis: Therapeutic Intervention
www.lovaas.com

Myles-A-Part: Supporting Families Facing Autism
www.mylesapart.com

The Autism Mosaic: Information and Support
www.theautismmosaic.blogspot.com

Summit Learning Center: Therapeutic Intervention
www.summitlearningcenter.org

LaVergne, TN USA
20 April 2010
179769LV00002B/2/P